Praise for *Eat That Cookie!*

Healthcare, as a vocation, holds the promise of almost unparalleled job satisfaction. Unfortunately, the daily life of the healthcare worker also brings a unique combination of physical, emotional, and interpersonal challenges—long hours, sometimes difficult patients, uncooperative coworkers, stressful decisions—often leading to a negative and cynical work environment. We see the results in the form of poor patient service and high staff turnover.

For the past decade, Liz Jazwiec has committed her life to improving workplace culture, and her impact has been significant. In her new book, *Eat That Cookie!*, Liz takes aim at the negative mindset directly, offering a wealth of insight on the topic: how to recognize it, how to address it, and what to do when the inevitable "pushback" occurs. Applying her characteristic blend of humor and directness, Liz makes a strong case for personal accountability and provides practical strategies for aligning staff in a positive way.

A "must-read" for healthcare managers at all levels, this book is long overdue.

—William J. Hejna, Senior Principal-Health Innovation, Noblis, Inc., Chicago, IL

Is there anyone in healthcare who tells it straighte

In *Eat That Cookie!*, she pulls no punches, tells it like it is, and doesn't accept any excuses. In it, she tells her story of transformation from a slave to the negative to a believer in the positive with such honesty that you can't help but relate to it. She is proof to us all that with the right amount of determination and tenacity we can all change for the better, adapt to new expectations, and achieve breakthrough results.

Liz stands out as one of those unique individuals who can tell a story so that you'll never forget it and its all-important lessons. And with a sense of humor that is second to none, she does that on every page of *Eat That Cookie!* With this book, Liz helps those of us in healthcare remember the core values that drew us to serve others and urges us to celebrate that choice every day.

I'm so excited that Liz has finally put her stories and philosophy to paper. This book should be on the reading list of everyone in healthcare. It shows just how proud we should all be of what we do! Read it and keep it close by—you never know when you will need Liz's great humor and even better guidance to help you through a tough day!

—Becky Anthony, Iowa Hospital Association

Liz Jazwiec knows nurses. She knows their work, she knows their frustrations, and she knows how deeply they care about their patients. In *Eat That Cookie!*, by telling her stories, with a humor that every nurse can relate to (because, let's face it, we've all been there!), she helps nurses see that their work extends far beyond their clinical expertise. Liz reminds us that nurses can reduce patient anxiety, establish patient confidence, and provide care that makes them feel truly cared for and totally satisfied with the patient experience.

In *Eat That Cookie!*, Liz also brilliantly uses her gift of humor to tell her own story about how she moved from a place of negativity to a place of ownership and positivity. (She's a natural storyteller who could have had an amazing career as a stand-up comedienne if she hadn't become a nurse!) She reminds us all what an important role we play in assuring an optimum experience for our patients. If you want to improve the quality of care your patients receive, read this book. Its lessons are invaluable for anyone in healthcare!

—Ruth Walton, RN, MS, Regional Chief Nurse Executive, Vanguard Health Systems

EAT
THAT
COOKIE!

Make **Workplace Positivity** Pay Off...
For Individuals, Teams and Organizations

Liz Jazwiec

Published by:
Fire Starter Publishing
913 Gulf Breeze Parkway, Suite 6
Gulf Breeze, FL 32561
Phone: 850-934-1099
Fax: 850-934-1384
www.firestarterpublishing.com

ISBN: 978-0-9840794-4-5

Library of Congress Control Number: 2009934547

Printed in the United States of America

I dedicate this book to:

My husband, Frank, who makes all that I do possible by supporting me with love, patience, kindness, strength, and, most importantly, humor. He is my rock as well as my gentle place to land. He encourages me to take things lightly and makes me laugh every day.

My Dad, who unfortunately passed away before this was written. He taught me that with a positive attitude, openness to opportunity, and hard work I could accomplish anything. He helped me realize that different is not wrong and that compassion and kindness go a long way in this world.

My Mom, my biggest fan, who keeps me grounded but never stops encouraging me to reach for the stars. She teaches me by her own example that in life, acknowledging things for what they are and accepting them with grace and humor will get you through anything.

My sister, Donna, whose steadfast support means more to me than she will ever realize. She blends success with compassion and belief in her convictions with an open mind and heart, and she is the only person I know who rivals Frank for downright silliness.

My nieces, Cathy and Lauren, and my nephew, Tyler, who each in their own very special way are ready to make the world a more positive place. I cannot wait to see what these extraordinary young people contribute and accomplish in their lives.

And finally, to everyone working in healthcare. Thank you for consistently reminding me that there's no greater profession in this world. No one works harder than you do. No one touches (and improves!) lives the way you do. You are my constant reminder that there is so much about healthcare that is good and right. You inspire me daily and for that I am forever and truly grateful!

Table of Contents

Foreword

When I listen to Liz speak, my first thought is, *I hope they're listening.* Then it quickly moves to, *She is talking about me.* Liz has the uncanny ability to combine her unique use of humor, stories, and analogies with passion and experience to help all who listen be more effective in our jobs and be better human beings. Now with *Eat That Cookie!* even more people can be touched directly and indirectly.

I am not sure of the exact date that I met Liz. I know it was in 1993 when I started working at Holy Cross Hospital (HCH) in Chicago as senior vice president and Liz was the director of the Emergency Department (ED). Early on in my tenure at HCH, I was assigned by the CEO, Mark Clement, to improve patient satisfaction. Not knowing much about how to do this, I quickly went to my usual game plan of studying the situation, diagnosing the issues, and creating a work plan. After all, it could not be that tough. I was wrong. Today, I know that to create a great patient experience means getting everyone on the same page doing the same things always. Not an easy task. Ignorance is bliss at times, so we got to work.

I am sure Liz shook her head yes to the plan. I know now she then went back to work with the attitude, *Here we go again, another talking head, another buzzword, another program. Why can't they leave us alone so we can get our work done?* As the work progressed, most of the leaders implemented steps in their areas and made steady gains in patient satisfaction—except in the Emergency Department and a few inpatient units.

Mark and I sat down and reviewed the progress and the decision was made to remove the leaders who had not made expected progress from their leadership roles. There were four leaders on the list to be let go. As we worked through the name of replacements for those leaving, a challenge came up. We just did not have anyone to replace Liz at that time. I argued that we should still let Liz go. Mark (who was right) said, "Let's give her 90 more days." Knowing I was on the losing side on that call, I did get Mark to agree that we could put Don Dean in her office. Don was our leader in outpatient services. He was getting great results, and I felt that this way when Liz failed, Don could step right in.

I found out I had misjudged Liz and the ED staff. Liz had survival skills and her staff loved her. When Liz told the staff that if things did not improve in 90 days she was gone, the staff rallied behind Liz, and results improved. Being skeptical, I would often ask Don about Liz. Being in her office, he kept telling me she was doing the right things and results would come. I had to be patient. Don was right; results did come. In this book you will read about that journey, what was learned, and much more.

Now move ahead to June of 1996. After three-and-a-half years at Holy Cross, I was leaving to be the administrator of Baptist Hospital, Inc., in Pensacola, Florida. I had come full circle in my relationship with Liz. The person I felt I could not live with, I now felt I could not live without.

Well, I have not had to live without Liz. I hired Liz as a consultant to help work with leaders and staff at Baptist and today Liz is a key part of Studer Group.* I am blessed to have Liz in my life since 1993. Those who have heard Liz will agree on the positive impact she has on the lives of so many people.

I trust you will agree after reading *Eat That Cookie!* It is more than a bite but a whole meal on feeding our passion and soul in this journey to make ourselves and our organizations better.

Quint Studer

Introduction

I learned the importance of creating positive workplaces the hard way. During the first 18 years of my career, I had an extremely negative attitude. Over time, something happened to me that changed my outlook, my attitude, my life. When I was forced into a customer service initiative at the hospital where I used to work, I learned how to walk away from negativity and what I call "victim-thinking." Because of the role that service initiative played in shaping my personal behavior, you will read a lot about service in this book. For me, excellent service and positive workplaces are intertwined, and I believe as you read you will also recognize the connection between the two.

Let me set the stage. I was working as the director of the ED of Holy Cross Hospital, an inner-city hospital on the South Side of Chicago. It sits right next to Marquette Park, a three-square-mile urban park that has some of its own permanent residents…know what I mean? We were one of the back-up providers of choice for the Cook County Jail, and though we were not the designated trauma center in the area, we were a "beep-beep drop center."

I can hear some of you thinking now: *What's a "beep-beep drop center"*? (I can also imagine others nodding knowingly.) Basically, we were serving an area of

Chicago that had a lot of gang activity. And as you all know, gang members are in high-risk occupations. They often find themselves shot or stabbed, but they don't like to call 911—mostly because it tends to attract the attention of the police.

Anyway, gangs have come up with their own little triage system. When one of their colleagues is suddenly injured, they throw the person into the car, drive to the closest hospital, pull up onto the apron of the ED entrance, throw the body out onto the concrete, honk the horn a couple times so the staff knows there has been a fresh delivery, and then they speed away. See? Beep-beep drop.

The bottom line? We were in a rough part of town. And our clientele weren't always Chicago's most upstanding of citizens.

When I started at Holy Cross in 1991, it was an organization with problems. It was deeply troubled financially. And its reputation in the community wasn't the best. In fact, many people had taken to referring to the hospital by some less than favorable nicknames.

And perhaps the most telling evidence of the hospital's troubles was that back in 1991, 95 percent of the people who worked at Holy Cross would not go there for their own healthcare. That's right. Ninety-five percent of the people who worked there would say when they got sick, "What are you thinking? I'm not going to Holy Cross!" Our employees had lost faith in their own organization. That's really bad, isn't it?

Holy Cross is sponsored by a small group of Lithuanian nuns. I'm not making that up. The Sisters of St. Casimir. Yep, St. Casimir. I have to tell you that I was born and raised Catholic, and I never once heard of that saint. In fact, at first I thought they were saying the Sisters of St. *Cashmere*. I thought to myself, *Ooh, we're going to wear really nice uniforms in this hospital. Beats the Daughters of Charity. The Sisters of St. Cashmere: a whole group of nuns devoted to good wool...* Got to love a good nun pun!

In 1992, the Good Sisters decided it was time to bring in new executives. They brought in Mark Clement to be our new CEO. Mark had a strong service sense, and not too long after he arrived, he hired a man by the name of Quint Studer.

Quint was there to provide us with some much needed help in the area of customer service. We needed someone to help us refocus. And we needed it badly. How badly? In October of 1993, we were in the 14th percentile of hospitals in terms of patient satisfaction as scored on a national survey tool. Now, as you all know, that's not good. However, we had spent the first five years we were surveying our patients in the 5th percentile. Five years in the 5th percentile! When our score went up to the 14th percentile, some of us were actually ready to write on our résumés: *Tripled patient satisfaction scores.*

The administrative team got together and tried to decide what the goals for the hospital should be. They said maybe we should shoot for the 50th percentile. But then Quint challenged them and said, "Can we really be a provider of choice with only average service?" So the decision was handed down. The goal was for us to end our fiscal year, which was in June, in the 75th percentile. In other words, we had nine months to go from the 14th to the 75th percentile. (Yikes!)

We tried to hire some consultants to help us, but no one would take the job. They told us what we were trying to do was impossible. They said, "You're going to demoralize your staff. You've set a goal that's too high."

But Quint was unfazed. He didn't listen to those "experts." Instead he started our service challenge by forming eight customer service teams. We named them—wait for it—"Customer Service Commandos." They were different from anything any of us had ever seen before. First of all, we didn't spend the first month arguing about the name. Normally, there would have been objections like: *Should we really call ourselves the Commandos? Isn't that a negative term? Or, Is it right to use military terms to decide what we do in healthcare? Blah, blah, blah.* Taking a month to decide on a committee name just wasn't in Quint's M.O.

The other thing that was different about the Commandos was that we had to meet every week, and every week we had to have a result. A result a week for eight teams—that's a lightning pace in healthcare, isn't it? A result a week! Needless to say, it was a horrible time at our hospital. After all, you know how much we like change in healthcare. I'd walk into a room and everything would be turned around. "What happened?" I would ask. And the staff would say, "Commandos." To which I always responded with a sneer and an eye roll.

So, a lot was changing and it was happening fast. Eight things a week, 32 things a month, 100 things a quarter, and half of them failed. Oh, we're afraid of that in healthcare, aren't we? We hate when things fail. Well, we half hate it. The other half kind of enjoys getting to tell people, "Told you so. Told you that change would never work in our department!" But even with half of the initiatives failing, implementing 50 of them a quarter was faster than our organization had ever moved before.

People have since asked me, "What was your strategic plan?" And I always say, "Well, apparently, our strategic plan was to run around like chickens with their heads cut off." We were faced with an ultimate goal that seemed impossible, to go from the 14th percentile to the 75th percentile in nine months. How long does it take an organization to write a strategic plan, anyway? Nine months? Ten months? Two years? We didn't have a plan because we didn't have time for one. We were just doing whatever we could do. Novel idea, huh?

And as it turned out, we didn't hit our goal in nine months. We reached it in *six*. By March of 1994, we were in the 75th percentile, and we finished that year in the 94th percentile. Yes, we moved from the 14th percentile to the 94th percentile in only nine months. That's quite an impressive jump. We won recognition and awards. March of 1994 was a remarkably happy time at the hospital. We reached a goal that healthcare industry "experts" had told us would be impossible, and we did it three months ahead of schedule. And I've got to tell you, despite all those dire predictions, the staff was anything but demoralized. Most people had never been more proud of the work they were doing.

Okay, full disclosure: It was a happy time at the hospital…except for in the ER. Want to take a guess where our scores were? It was a single digit. Eight! We were in the 8th percentile, and I was so twisted at that time I was actually proud of it. I would walk around the hospital bragging that we were the only department actually working! I'd say, "Well now, that finally proves one thing. Apparently, we are the only department working. Everybody else has time to do all this customer service, nicey-nicey fluff stuff. Meanwhile, we're down here saving lives, stamping out disease."

Then, Quint called me into his office. He said, "Liz, we want to make your exit from the organization as graceful as possible. So, unless there is a dramatic change in service, we're going to transition you out over the next 90 days." Two days later he moved the director of Ambulatory Care and the hospital's golden boy, Don Dean, into my office. He was the hospital's superstar. You know the type. Perfect in every way. Happy, happy, happy…ALL THE TIME!

Don Dean and I are great friends now. But let me tell you, it was a tough first year…for him. Now, in some hospitals, Ambulatory Care and ED go together, don't they? Don was the director of Ambulatory Care and they moved him in. Now in case you didn't catch my wording earlier, they didn't just move him into the same suite as me. They moved him into *my office*. When your replacement moves into your office, it's a sign, and not a good one.

So I went to my ED staff and I said, "You guys, we have to focus on patient satisfaction." Day 90 came and went. On Day 85 I gave them a pep talk, "Come on, you guys! Customer satisfaction, that's where it's at." (As you can imagine, this had a huge impact.) Day 80 came and went. And somewhere around day 75, I finally confessed to them. I said, "You guys, if we don't fix patient satisfaction by June 1st, I'm fired." And fortunately for me, they liked me. Otherwise, they might have said, "*Oh, really, Liz? That would be a shame. We surely would hate to see that happen. Yeah, that'd be a real shame.*"

So then the ED staff, being the sweethearts that they were, took on this attitude, like, "Oh, you want to see service, do you? Want to see service? Oh, we'll give you service." They began a customer service strategy that I call "simpering"—basically using a tone with patients that falls somewhere between sweet and sarcastic. I'd walk into the treatment area and people with fake smiles on their faces would be saying things like, "Oh no, we don't mind doing that for you. After all, that's why we're here. We're here to serve you."

The first time I heard this I thought, *Well, that's that. I'm fired for sure.*

But we learned something in the ED during those 90 days. You know what it was? People will respond to insincere kindness!

And we learned something else too. Up until this point, we in the ED had been convinced we had the most difficult clientele in the country, the most demanding families, the most obnoxious patients. Our specialty seemed to be people who were unappreciative, people who were difficult to take care of. But when we started to treat them differently something happened. They started treating *us* differently, and I learned something as a leader. I gradually started to understand how important it is for us to have pride and respect for everything we do in our day-to-day work lives in healthcare.

1

Customer Service + Job Satisfaction = Pride: A Formula for Positivity

For many years of my healthcare career I resisted service. I did so for two reasons. Number one, I just liked the sport of resisting something so many people were up in arms about. I decided I didn't like it, and I didn't want to do it. I really did not have a logical reason. It just bugged me, so I did everything I could to avoid it. Now, I don't know about you, but for many of us, if we don't have a rational explanation for why we want to resist doing this or that in our work lives, we pull out what I call the "professional" trump card. In fact, I used to use it pretty frequently. A boss or superior would ask me to do something, and I would reply, "That insults me professionally!" Now, c'mon, some of you have done the same thing…admit it!

I used the trump card on Quint one day. He was lecturing me on service and the ED's scores, and frankly, I was tired of it. So I told him, "This service stuff INSULTS ME PROFESSIONALLY!"

And he said, "TAKE A PILL!"

"Take a pill?" I questioned him, somewhat shocked. (The trump card had never failed me like that before.)

"Yes, Liz. Get over it," he said and left the room.

Well, you can probably all guess the rest of that story. I did eventually get over it. And to be honest, feeling insulted was not the main reason I resisted service.

As a leader in healthcare, I resisted addressing the issue of service primarily because I felt I was already asking my team to go above and beyond the call of duty. I didn't think I could ask them to do even more. I thought, *How can I go to a group of people who I know are already working very hard every day, and ask them to do yet another thing that's going to make their jobs even more difficult? They are already working under difficult circumstances every day: inadequate staffing, a census that's off the walls, equipment that's breaking down, computers that aren't cooperating. How can I go to them and ask them to worry about yet another problem?*

But then I discovered something about healthcare: Focusing on service does not make the job more difficult. It makes it more rewarding. And, though there aren't a lot of things I can say about healthcare today with absolute certainty, that is one of them. Focusing on service makes the job better. It makes people feel proud about their work. It makes for a much more positive work environment. And that's what we need in healthcare.

If It Makes You Happy, It Can't Be That Bad

I'm concerned when I go around the country today talking to people in healthcare and they're miserable. I think to myself, *How are they going to make it another one or two years, let alone another five or ten, if people are so miserable today? How much negativity can we withstand?*

And people say, "Well, Liz, what do you expect? We're overworked. We're understaffed. We're going through constant change. Healthcare is a very difficult place to be." Yes, it is. But it's going to be difficult for the rest of our careers. For the rest of our careers, we're going to be challenged to find good, talented people to come work with us. For the rest of our careers, we're going to be challenged financially. For the rest of our careers, we're going to go through change. But I don't think it's okay to be miserable for the rest of our careers! I think we need to tap back into those things that helped us fall in love with healthcare when we first started out.

For most of my career, I thought my team's motto was, "If you don't make me happy, I can't make the customer happy. If I'm not a happy nurse, I can't have a happy patient. You don't make me happy. I can't make them happy."

But that's not what happened in our ED.

Remember, those nurses I mentioned earlier were mad. They were not happy! We kind of had to shove them into doing the right thing. But once they started to do it, they started to feel better about their work. I've been in many, many healthcare organizations over the last 12 years, and I now understand that in healthcare, employee satisfaction has little to do with the parking lot, the benefit plan, or the staff schedules.

> Employee satisfaction boils down to knowing how we make a difference and how the work we do has purpose and meaning. And when people believe in the work they're doing, when they understand how the work they do is important, that's when they are satisfied. And that is when we move from negative organizational cultures to positive ones.

I think the biggest crisis we're facing in healthcare today is that the people working in it no longer feel heroic. And that's a shame because they should. I truly believe we are blessed to work in a field in which we can at any moment turn a corner and make a difference in someone's life. And we should feel heroic. My definition of a hero is someone who is remembered fondly by somebody else for the rest of their lives. In healthcare, we have the opportunity to be a hero every day. Leaders must help our teams remember that. Because when people feel heroic, it is amazing what they can accomplish.

The problem is that people working in healthcare do great things all the time, but they rarely feel heroic. They don't walk through the door at the end of the day believing that they made a difference. In fact, I find that people in healthcare today are so desensitized to feeling great about their work that even when they are told that they did a great job, it still doesn't resonate with them.

Stop and Take a Picture

Not too long ago, I was doing an all-day Nurses Week presentation in Boston when a nurse approached me during the break. She said, "Liz, something happened to me about eight months ago that I didn't think was a big deal until I heard you speak about heroes today." So I asked her what happened, and she told me her story:

Back in September, she went to her daughter's very first ever parent-teacher conference. At the time, her husband was out of town on business, and she was going to the meeting by herself, so her mother came over to watch her daughter. That particular day had been one of *those* days at work. As a result, she got home late, jumped in the shower, put on some fresh, clean clothes and got to the school as fast as she could. She was the last mom to enter the classroom, but fortunately the teacher was not in the room yet. She plopped down in the first empty seat she saw, and just as she sat, the woman sitting next to her turned to her and said, "Oh my gosh! It's YOU!"

And the nurse looked at her and deadpanned, "Why, yes, yes, it is."

Then the woman said, "I have your picture in my wallet!"

Ewwww, the nurse thought, *Who is this lady?*

And the woman continued, "You work in Neonatal Intensive Care. I remember you were pregnant the last time I saw you. Our kids must be in the same class!"

And with that the woman reached down into her purse and pulled out a picture of the nurse, very pregnant, holding her baby.

I looked at the nurse standing in front of me, telling this story, and asked her, "And you didn't think that was a big deal?!?"

"Nope," she answered. "I didn't really think about it, until I heard you speak today."

"Well, let me tell you something," I offered. "If someone keeps your picture in their wallet for five years, IT'S A BIG DEAL!"

Now, I am not nuts. I know that the picture was in the woman's wallet mostly because of the baby—not the nurse. I am not yet so crazy that I am unable to get that. But I also know there is a reason that mom carried that specific picture around for five years. I don't know the exact reason, but I can guess. Maybe the first pictures of her baby elicit more worry than joy, maybe they preferred the casual pose instead of the more formal ones taken by the hospital, or maybe it was taken on the first good day they had in the NICU. Perhaps it was the first time they had hope for their daughter. We can't know for sure the real reason why, but I do know this: That woman recognized that nurse as soon as she walked into the door. The nurse wasn't wearing a uniform and she wasn't pregnant anymore, but that mom remembered her right away. She remembered because that nurse made a difference in her life.

How sad that the nurse didn't get it! She didn't get it in the classroom when it happened that evening, and I guarantee you she didn't get it the day the picture was taken.

In fact, maybe on the day it happened, those parents were bugging her. Maybe they were saying, "Oh, come on! Take a picture—it will be fun!"

The Nurse: "Love to, but I am very busy right now."

The Parents: "How busy could you be?"

The Nurse: "Very sick babies to care for."

The Parents: "How sick could they be?"

The Nurse: "*NEONATAL INTENSIVE CARE*—that is how sick they are!"

The Parents: "Oh, c'mon, it will just take a minute. Please take a picture. It won't take long. Take a picture, just one. It will be fun! Please, just one picture."

The Nurse: "Okay, fine! Take the picture."

Back then she didn't realize that she was making a difference. And if she hadn't heard me that day, not only would she have missed out on feeling good about that encounter she had at the parent-teacher conference, but she would have missed out on feeling good about her work for years to come.

From now on how do you think she is going to feel when parents ask her to take a picture with their babies? I think totally different. And I am guessing that now she drives home at the end of a crazy day and thinks to herself, "Wow, the place was up for grabs, but at least I had a chance to stop and take a picture with that family!"

I am passionate about restoring pride in healthcare. We do great work, and we deserve to feel great about it. Every day, we do wonderful things. Every day, we deserve to be proud of ourselves.

Stop Beating Up on Healthcare

Surprisingly, when I talk about restoring pride in healthcare, sometimes I get pushback from the audience. They say things like, "You know, it is hard to feel good about our work when the media is so mean to us!" But I understand the media can be mean. And then I hear, "And this community, they have very long memories. You know, God forbid anything goes wrong. People talk about it for years and years, and they keep sharing the stories so the bad tales just go on and on!"

No doubt they do. But I am going to tell you that there is no one harder on healthcare than the people working in it.

We come to work every day and we bash it, trash it, and kick it around. Then, we go home and we bash it, trash it, and kick it around some more. Sometimes we are even lucky enough to get invited to a party. And it's, "Yippee! More people we can make feel sorry for us because we work in healthcare!" And then we bash it, trash it, and kick it around again.

STOP THAT! We have to stop it. We do wonderful work. If we are ever going to create a positive work environment, we have to stop talking trash about healthcare. We are blessed to work in an environment where we can truly make a difference. We need to embrace that, feel great about it, and share it with others.

I know healthcare is tough. Oh, how I know! I understand that you probably can't work much harder than you already are. But pride is what can give you the strength you need to get through those tough times at work and realize that although the work can be challenging, it is also extremely rewarding. And one thing that positive workplaces all share is that everyone working in them has a sense of pride about what they are accomplishing.

Without a doubt, I know you know you have these things happening in your organization every single day. No organization can excel in service if its employees don't feel pride for what they are doing. Organizations that sustain excellence in service have learned how to celebrate and recognize their heroes as a matter of practice.

I think the most compelling reason for us to focus on service is because it makes us feel good about the work we do. Yes, it's in your hospital's mission and vision statements. Yes, the experts will tell you that it's good for the bottom line and makes good business sense. Yes, I've learned the hard way that if it's important to your CEO, you'd better figure out a way to do it. But I think for those working in healthcare today, the most compelling reason to focus on service is that it makes us feel better. It makes us fall in love with healthcare all over again. It makes us proud of what we do!

Reclaiming Our Birthright

Healthcare was created to make people feel better. Even in its most basic, original form, it made people less anxious and more comfortable. It made a difference. For those of us in healthcare today, making people feel better is our birthright. Over the years some people have argued this point with me. They say, "Actually, Liz, healthcare was started to heal and cure." My reply to them is always, "Uh-uh, you are wrong. When healthcare first began, we didn't know how to heal and cure. All those first caretakers could do is make people more comfortable, help them feel better, and do a lot of praying that they hoped would make a difference."

Now don't get me wrong, I am very grateful that over the years we have learned how to heal and cure. But in healthcare making people feel better is our birthright, and we need to reclaim it! No other industry should be better than us at delivering its service with care and compassion.

And you know what? I'm tired of learning about service from other industries. I have for too long, and I know we will continue to do so until we reclaim our birthright of delivering a service with care and compassion. Until we reclaim that birthright, we are forced to look to folks in other industries. Disney is a wonderful example. Marriott is a good example. But I'm a little tired of hearing about them. I'm tired of hearing people talk about Southwest Airlines, not that I don't like the company and its people. Though, I must admit, I'm not quite tired of Nordstrom. I go there every chance I get, and I keep trying to write it off as a business expense. But I'm just wondering where is healthcare in all of this?

We do great work every day. We deserve to feel proud of the work we do. Reclaiming our birthright of delivering a service with care and compassion is one more step we can take on the path to making ourselves stronger, passionate, and better armed to face the future. Healthcare is not going to get any easier, and we know we can't work much harder. Restoring our pride in what we do will furnish us with the stamina we need to face whatever the future holds for us.

Delivering services with care and compassion: Once we reclaim that birthright, the rewards will be huge. We'll see an improvement in morale. Can you imagine working in a team where everyone has pride in their work? Not only will that create a positive work environment, but we will see people fall in love with healthcare all over again.

2

Declare Victim-Thinking DOA

Without a doubt one of the biggest challenges healthcare workers face today is victim-thinking. Once you start practicing this "deadly sin," it can be a very difficult habit to break. It poisons you. Worse, it renders you incapable of being successful.

Once again, I speak from experience. You see, I am an ex-smoker *and* an ex-victim.

I am not one of those judgmental reformed smokers. You know the kind. Despite the fact they themselves used to smoke more than a pack a day, they now condemn everyone else who does it. In fact, I still miss smoking. I liked it, and when people ask, *Don't you feel better?* the answer is actually *no*! In fact, when I quit 13 years ago, I told myself that I was just taking a break. If I am lucky enough to live to be 80, I am going to start smoking again…and maybe not just cigarettes!

I am a much less tolerant ex-victim than I am an ex-smoker. In fact, now that I've squashed my own victim-thinking, I am relentless. I hate it when I hear people say they can't do something, or that their organization is different, or that they've tried something and it doesn't work...blah, blah, blah. I especially worry when I hear words like that coming out of the mouths of leaders.

One of the best lessons Quint Studer ever taught me was that you can't take your team further than you have taken yourself. And if you repeatedly give in to victim-thinking, you will be stopped dead in your tracks.

Victim-thinking is dangerous because those who give in to it come up with just one reason why they can't be successful or why they won't reach this or that goal, and then they give up. Good leaders don't let that happen on their watch.

A good coach doesn't go into a locker room at halftime with a team that is getting the stuffing kicked out of them and say, "Those other guys are huge. Don't worry about getting the ball. Don't worry about scoring any points. Let's just pray we all make it back to the bus without anybody getting hurt!"

A good coach would go into that locker room and say, "Wow, we are really up against a good team today, but I know I have the right people with me in this locker room today. Let's get out there, and go get 'em!" Sure, his team might not win. But at least when the final buzzer has sounded they'll know they tried their best. They'll know their coach believes in them.

Unfortunately, in the healthcare world, I hear leaders saying things very similar to the former coaching example all the time. They tell their busy staff, "I know it's busy. Hang in there! Just do whatever you have to do to make it through the day!"

Of course, these leaders are only making a difficult situation worse. They might think that they are being sympathetic or helpful, but they're not. They're just reinforcing victim-thinking and allowing their staff to be less than they can be. (Hey, wonder why the Army doesn't use "Be less than you can be" as their slogan?) To be a good leader, you must create a positive work environment by eliminating the victim mentality in yourself and your team.

Facing the Truth

One time, when I was working at Holy Cross, I was asked to speak at our hospital's department head meeting. The ED had gotten into the 90th percentile and I was going to present our success story.

As I was preparing for the presentation, I remembered something else that I had learned from Quint: Good leaders take responsibility for their team's failures, but they attribute successes to the team as a whole. So I asked two of my staff members to be a part of my presentation. It was supposed to be a short presentation, only about 10 minutes long. My plan was that I would open and close the presentation, and I would have the two staff members do the main part.

Quint came to visit me about 5:00 p.m. the evening before my presentation. He asked me if I was prepared, and I told him that I was. I told him that I had asked two members of my staff to join me and that we were all set.

Then he asked, "Don't you think you ought to tell the group what really happened?"

"I am," I said. "We are going to tell the whole story."

"Don't you think you need to tell the audience exactly what barriers existed?" he pressed.

"We *are*," I insisted. "We are prepared to discuss all the things we did."

And finally, he got right down to the point. "Don't you think the group deserves to know that YOU were the biggest problem? And that until you changed as a leader, the team was never going to move forward?" he asked.

I just looked at him. When Quint suggests something, it is like The Godfather suggesting something. It isn't really a suggestion so much as it is a command.

He left my office, and I was ticked! I called my friend Mark Albarian in California. He always gives me great advice, and he had been advising me throughout all my struggles at the hospital.

"You are not going to believe what they want me to do now!" I whined. "It is not bad enough that I have been jumping through hoops for the last nine months! Now they want me to stand up in front of my colleagues and friends and say, 'My name is Liz, and I am a LOUSY leader.'"

I expected Mark to be outraged, but he wasn't. "Oh, Liz," he said. "You've come this far. Just do it. Don't fight unnecessary battles."

So, I begrudgingly agreed. After I spoke with Mark, I told my team members they could stay home the next day. I was going to go it alone on the presentation.

I got up that day in front of all my friends and coworkers and started my story. I told them that as a leader I could not take my team further than I had taken myself and that somewhere along the way I had gotten stuck. I said that I had to change before my team began to see success…blah, blah, blah. As I presented, I looked at the audience. Some people had their jaws open, eyes staring in disbelief; others had tears in their eyes. I imagine those people were probably thinking, *They finally got to Liz!*

In retrospect, that presentation was the start of my speaking career. Giving up my victim-thinking had truly opened new doors for me. I was no longer going to stand in the way of my own success or that of my department.

The Life of the Victim

Some of the hallmarks of victim-thinking are denial, blame, and rationalization. I was a classic case. I tapped into all of those traits when I was coming up with reasons why our customer service scores weren't better. We used a mailed survey to measure our responses, and I had a whole boatload of reasons why our outcomes weren't better. I used just about every tool in the victim thinker's bag to explain our bad results.

First, I denied that we were really all that bad. Sure, we were in the 8th percentile, I reasoned, but our score is a 78. And 78 is not really failing. It is more like a solid "C."

Then when denial didn't work, I tried blame. When you work in an ED, blame is a great tool to use because you can point the finger at a different department every week. It was never my ED's fault. It was security, admitting, the doctors, the lab. Or maybe it was housekeeping. Perhaps they are in cahoots with some of the nursing units and are hiding clean beds so we can't get anyone admitted from the ED.

Eventually, though, blame started to wear thin. Then I would pull out the big gun, RATIONALIZATION.

I loved rationalization. I was the queen of rationalization. I mean, c'mon, my name is in the middle of the word. RationaLIZation. I was an absolute pro at rationalizing why our scores were so bad.

I would start with what I felt was the most obvious reason for the bad scores. "We actually do a great job at customer service," I would say. "Our patients just don't realize it." I guess I was talking about that "stealth" service—you know, the kind that's so specialized only an expert can detect it.

Next, I rationalized it must be the survey tool. We weren't getting a big enough response rate because there were too many questions on the survey. I was certain that the questions were asked in the wrong order and that there was a clear bias against the nursing staff.

When that didn't work, I pointed the finger at the patients. It was very clear to me. We were working in a tough neighborhood! We were taking care of homeless people! We were bathing them, feeding them, clothing them, and then sending them back out on the streets! *Of course* they weren't happy! And what about the criminals? We were taking care of people who were handcuffed to their stretchers. Oh, and the drug seekers! They'd come looking for drugs and then we wouldn't give them any. These people weren't likely to give us a high score!

Can you guess what was wrong with all those rationalizations?

It took me six months to figure out that homeless people didn't have mailboxes!

Six months to realize that there wasn't anyone walking around Cook County Jail asking the inmates to fill out the survey. And six months to discover that our drug seekers didn't always give us the correct contact information. I mean, why would they? "Hey, you want to find me? This is where I can be tracked down when you want to bring someone in for trying to illegally obtain prescription drugs."

Those patients I was pointing the finger at were not the ones filling out our patient satisfaction surveys. Maybe you got it right away, but, me, I am not that smart.

At the time, though, I didn't want to think about any of that. The first reason I could come up with to justify our lack of success was good enough for me, no matter what it was. And *that* is the most dangerous thing about victim-thinking.

You don't have to have a good reason for your failure, or even one that makes sense, as long as you and your staff are willing to believe it. And once you believe it, you are dead in the water.

Stop Being the Victim

To create a positive work environment, we have to eliminate victim-thinking. We have to. And once it's gone the outcome will be remarkable. Denial is replaced with results, blame with gratitude, and rationalization with success.

Trust me, once you and your team know what success feels like, you will never want to go back to victim-thinking again.

One of the best gifts Quint gave me was teaching me how to stop thinking like a victim. He taught me that by example. He never let me or my staff give in to victimhood. And as a result, Holy Cross Hospital—despite all of those reasons I gave that should have kept us from being successful—began receiving awards honoring its great service.

Eliminating victim-thinking from your mindset and the mindsets of those you lead is the best gift you can give to yourself and the people you work with. Once you do, people start to feel like winners. And in healthcare, as hard as we work, everyone deserves to feel like a winner. We deserve to be successful. And there is nothing that promotes a positive work environment more than ongoing success.

3

Changing Their Behavior: Yes, You *Can* Have an Accountable Workplace

Leaders, this chapter is for you! And when I say leaders, I am not just talking about managers, directors, and administrators. Leaders are everywhere, both formal and informal. So if you are a preceptor, you're a leader. If you are assigned charge nurse on the weekends, you're a leader. If you are head tech on the afternoon shift in the pharmacy, you got it...you're a leader!

As I travel the country, meeting with healthcare professionals, I spend a lot of time talking about what individuals and teams need to do in order to create positive work environments. And while I do not believe that it is solely the leader's responsibility to eliminate all negativity on their team and make sure everyone is in a good mood every day, I do believe that the most important thing a leader can do to create a positive work environment is to hold everyone accountable to the same standards. A fair workplace is a positive workplace.

When I talk to people at various organizations, they often tell me that they have coworkers who could use an attitude adjustment. If everyone had the "right" attitude, they say, everything would be okay. If only there were an "attitude fairy" who could fly over the workplace waving her wand and spreading sunshine and roses, right?

Actually, in my years working in the healthcare world, I've discovered that it is people's behaviors, not their attitudes, that create a negative work environment. When you start holding people accountable for those negative behaviors, that is when people start to change their negative behaviors into good ones, and as a result everyone gets to enjoy a more positive, productive workplace.

Accountability: The Path to a Positive Workplace

If you want to create a positive work environment, you have to start holding people accountable for their behaviors. *But we can't hold people accountable for their behaviors,* you're probably thinking. Or at least, that's what I always hear when I bring up the subject during my speeches. People tell me accountability isn't part of their company culture. Or they say HR won't let them.

To that I say, "Wrong!" We do hold people accountable for their behaviors inside our organizations. It is just that we currently hold them accountable for *some* behaviors and not others.

Most organizations are very good at holding people accountable for behaviors pertaining to cost or quality. But we are not so good at holding people accountable for other ones—like those pertaining to customer service or (gasp!) morale.

My theory is that leaders hold people accountable for the behaviors that they are comfortable confronting people about. For example, most leaders don't bat an eye at talking to employees about how their behaviors are costing the company money. Most workplaces have rules about what time you can clock in, whether you punch a clock, swipe a badge, or log in on a computer. The usual requirement is that an employee does not clock in more than seven minutes before her scheduled work time. So if someone starts a shift at 8:00 a.m. the soonest she can clock in would be 7:53 a.m.

Let's say there is a new person working at your organization. He is eager to demonstrate not only his punctuality but the fact that he is at work earlier than most and ready to get down to business. So he clocks in at 7:30 a.m. every morning. His leader is going to have to have a chat with him. But it will be very simple. She'll probably pull him aside and say, "Joe, I am happy that you are here early every day. I think that it's great that you are eager to get to work, but you can't clock in before 7:53."

That's it. No drama. The leader didn't need to be coached about what to say. She probably didn't worry over it the night before. She isn't tormented about talking to him because the behavior is one she is comfortable discussing. She's asking him to abide by a commonly accepted practice that has been in place for a long time. She feels completely justified in enforcing the behavior so there is no unpleasantness associated with confronting Joe about it.

So, cost is pretty easy, accountability-wise. Quality is another no-brainer. Most leaders are so comfortable holding people accountable for quality behaviors that they might not even realize how often they do it.

For example, let's say a nurse leader is walking past a patient's room and she sees a nurse who is getting ready to start an IV drop the needle on the floor. The nurse picks it up, wipes it on her pant leg, blows on it a couple of times, and aims it at the patient's arm. That leader would and should fly into that room and stop her immediately. Then, in private, she will probably say, "I noticed that technique and that is a totally unacceptable behavior." The nurse may respond, "Oh, you noticed that did you? Funny you didn't notice how busy we are today. Two nurses called in sick and another staff member is down in special procedures with a patient. But no! You don't notice those things. You just notice me doing something wrong!"

Now is the leader going to say, "Wow, I guess you really are busy! Don't worry about it! Those pants were probably clean anyway!" Of course not! She knows the nurse's behavior was totally unacceptable so she won't have a problem pushing the issue. No matter how busy that nurse is she is always expected to give her patients the utmost quality of care. And the leader is comfortable in holding her to those standards of behavior.

Or consider another scenario. Let's say on that very same nursing unit a new service behavior was introduced. It requires staff to ask patients as they leave their room, "Is there anything else I can do for you? I'll make time." As the same leader walks past a room, she witnesses the same nurse leaving a room without asking the patient the service initiative question.

The leader approaches the nurse and says, "Pam, I noticed that you didn't ask your patient if there was anything else that you could do for him." Pam glares at her and says, "INTERESTING that you would notice that, when you seem to have failed to notice how busy we are here today! Two nurses called in sick and another staff member is down in special procedures with a patient. But nooooooo, you don't notice that. You just notice me doing something wrong!"

This time, however, the leader does back off. She says, "Wow, I guess you are really, really busy. Don't worry. I know next time you will do better."

Now I ask you, reader: *Will* the nurse do better next time? My guess is, no, she will not. Why? Because now she knows which behaviors she will be held accountable for and which ones she can slide on.

If a leader is not comfortable with a behavior, there is a slim chance that she will hold her team accountable for it. Slim to none—and "Slim" just left. The only solution is for leaders to get comfortable with discomfort. If the leader thinks a behavior is out of reach or unreasonable, it will be impossible for them to hold people accountable for the behavior. Every team knows what is important to their boss. If you send a message that it is okay to ignore a standard, then guess what! IT GETS IGNORED!

Here's one last example. Acme Hospital has a telephone answering standard. Based on the standard, those who answer the phone should give the department name, their name, and then ask, "How may I help you?"

One day Bill, the leader of 4West, a department at Acme, calls his unit and the unit clerk answers the phone with an abrupt, "4West." Now if Bill is comfortable holding his staff accountable for the phone answering standard, he will reply, "Mary, this is Bill. When you answer the phone on our unit, I expect to hear, '4West, this is Mary. How may I help you?'"

But on this occasion, Bill hears that curt "4West," and thinks, "Wow, it sounds like a crazy busy day on the unit. Today is not the day to get on Mary's case." However, being the good leader that he is, Bill doesn't ignore the problem. He just doesn't correct Mary at that very moment. Instead he takes out a pen and writes himself a note: *Discuss telephone answering policy at next department meeting.*

In theory, that approach might sound like a good idea, but who in that scenario is held accountable for their actions? No one! Mary is going to be at that meeting thinking, *It is about time Bill gets on all these people who never answer the phone the right way! I am the only one who follows the standard.*

Leaders *must* be resolute in holding people accountable to the appropriate standards of behavior, even when they are not yet completely comfortable with them themselves. Trust me, if you don't, your staff will quickly pick up on which behaviors they must adhere to and which ones you will let them get away with ignoring.

Your Organization, It Is A-Changin'

So, how do you make these behavioral changes stick at your organization? First, you have to be picky about which changes you want to implement.

You can't throw a list of 8-12 changes at your staff and expect them to be able to keep up with all of them. In fact, most people can change only 3-4 behaviors a year.

Think about your organization's behavioral changes the same way you think about your own personal New Year's resolutions. I love New Year's resolutions. I do them every year. Actually, I guess it might be more accurate to say, I love New Year's resolutions. I do the *same ones* every year! When it comes time to put together my list, I usually just copy my list from the previous year:

1. Lose weight.
2. Swear less.
3. Go to the gym.

Although, one year I did put a really tough one on my list. I decided in 2007 that I was going to be nicer to people in airports. For me this was a big deal. I am in an airport 3-4 times a week, and there are a lot of things that people do in airports that bug me. For example, I believe there ought to be a rule that says if someone walking ahead of you in an airport just stops for no apparent reason—I am walking, I am walking, STOP!—that we should be able to shove them.

Another thing that drives me nuts is people traveling with pillows. Most of the time the pillow-carriers are young people in their late teens to early 20s. I've asked some of them, "What's with the pillow? What pillow-less place are you traveling to?" Most of them tell me that they always travel with their very favorite pillow and that they can't sleep without it…blah, blah, blah.

Come on, people! By the time you get to your location, that pillow is going to be filthy! It's been dragged through security, propped up in airport bathrooms, and coated with creepy-crawly germs from the terminal's floor. YIKES! How can that be better?!? Perhaps, needless to say, I kept the resolution to be nicer to people in airports for only about six months. After that I just couldn't do it any more. But had there been someone there holding me accountable—maybe a New Year's Resolution Cop or a TSA-appointed "Be Nice" Officer—I may have had more success.

But, I digress. Let's get back to the topic at hand: changing negative behaviors. Problemo numero uno? Behaviors are hard to change. If Mary has been answering the phone with a curt, "4West," for 10 years, it is going to take her more than four weeks to change that behavior.

I know organizations that have tried to adopt 8-12 service standards in a given year and wonder why they are not seeing an improvement in customer satisfaction. I always ask them, "What kind of implementation strategy did you use? Did you introduce each one separately and wait until you had 80 percent compliance before introducing the next? Did you start slow and build?"

And they almost always reply, "No, we rolled them all out at once and made everyone sign the back of the new standards manual." Hmmm…Wonder why *that* didn't work?

Leaders have to remember to start slow. It takes a long time to change a behavior. Make sure you have 80 percent compliance on a changed behavior before moving to the next standard. By introducing standards one at a time, waiting for your staff to comply, and holding them accountable when they don't, you show them that the changes are important to you. As a result, they will make them important for them.

People are smart. If you move too fast, they know that all they have to do is lie low and wait for the newest fad to fade. And, in hospitals at least, many people work only three days a week. If the changes are focused on for only a month, that means your staff has to dodge the proposed change for only 12 days; then they are free to go back to business as usual.

Open Up and Say, "Hi!"

While I was at Holy Cross, one of our behavior initiatives was that we were all supposed to say "Hi" to those we passed in the hallway. It was a big deal when that change was implemented because the previous CEO, one of the Sisters of St. Casimir, did not allow talking in the halls. Ha! Can you believe that? It was a miracle that I was not fired on my first day.

So after years of no talking in the hallways, getting people to start saying "Hi" was a huge change. And in order to make sure it caught on, we knew we would have to enforce it, so we created what we called the Hello Police.

No, I am not kidding. I got a call from one of them one day:

Officer Hi said, "Kim is not saying 'Hi' in the hallways."

Oh, for Pete's sake, I thought to myself. But I knew the behavior had to be enforced so I called Kim into my office and begged her, "Will you please start saying 'Hi' in the hallways?"

She replied, "I AM BUSY SAVING LIVES!"

"Not in the hallways, you're not!" I snipped.

In the '90s when our "Hi" initiative was being implemented, it was an unusual standard for a hospital to be focusing on. One day at Holy Cross I received a call from a professor of medicine at the University of Chicago.

Now I am going to assume that most of you are familiar with the University of Chicago. It is an extremely prestigious university located on the South Side of Chicago. Now, if you know anything about Chicago, you know the South Side is pretty tough. Some people say, "Well, the South Side is just very blue collar." I beg to differ. It is more *no* collar!

In fact, I always thought it was kind of strange that such a well-renowned hallmark of higher education made its home on the South Side. And I must admit that there was always a little bit of tension between Holy Cross and U of C. Probably not on their part, but on ours, like we felt we were beneath them or not in the same league.

So it was really something for me on that day to receive a call from a professor of medicine from such a place. Our conversation went something like this:

Professor of Medicine: "I would like to get some information on your patient greeter program."

Me: "We don't have patient greeters." (My heart sank! We didn't use patient greeters because we didn't have the budget for it!)

Professor of Medicine: "Not greeter. *Greeting.* You use a very special greeting."

Now Perplexed, Me: "Um, we say 'Hi.'"

Professor of Medicine: "That's amazing! How did you ever do that?"

Still Perplexed, Me: "Um, we told people to say 'Hi.'"

Professor of Medicine: "Wow! Then what happened?" (I should add that he seemed genuinely excited about the concept. It sounded as if he was on the edge of his seat!)

Me: "They started saying 'Hi.'"

Professor of Medicine: "UNBELIEVABLE! I would LOVE to be able to teach this."

Me: "I think you can." (What I was really thinking was, *You have more degrees than a thermometer! I am pretty sure you can teach people how to say "Hi"!)*

The truth is the way people interact in the hallways of hospitals *is* a big deal. I can go into an organization and get a pretty good idea of its culture just by watching people pass each other. In organizations with a "good" attitude, staff members say "Hi" to each other, patients, and visitors in the hallways. Oops! There is that "attitude" word again. Why? Because most of the time, when you force a behavior change, an attitude change evolves from it. Not always, but most of the time, when a change is implemented with uniform compliance, the attitude follows.

As I said, for a long time before the "Hi" initiative, we were not allowed to talk in the hallways at Holy Cross Hospital.

Saying "Hi" to everyone we passed was a significant change. I guarantee you that if we had only announced the standard and waited four weeks for it to take hold, we would not have been successful in implementing it. Everyone would have just waited it out.

What's Fair Is Fair

When organizations approach change initiatives half-heartedly, it brings down the spirit of the team. People see the change as the "flavor of the month," or they wonder why they are being held accountable for a change when others aren't. Then it becomes a fairness issue.

In fact, change initiatives can lead to major complaints from staff members. When they are asked, "Are people treated fairly in this organization?" many respondents will say, "No." When my own staff would respond in that way, it used to surprise me. I thought fairness was about seniority when it came to scheduling vacations or working the holidays. It never occurred to me that failing to hold all staff accountable to new standards or policies could be viewed as my being unfair.

But I get it now. In order to create a great workplace, everyone has to be held accountable for their behaviors. Doing so levels the playing field. Everyone might not embrace or even like every policy change, regulation, or standard of behavior, but if all team members are held accountable for their actions, things feel fair, positive changes are implemented, and the workplace gets better and better.

4

Paralyzed by the Two Ps: How to Prevent Process and Perfection from Holding Your Organization Back

Most people believe that one of the reasons the workplace is such a drag is because we are so busy. But, actually, that's not true. Continuously experiencing a lack of results is what drags people down.

People are invigorated by accomplishing goals. It gives us a sense of success. That is a fact. But yet, we do things every day in the workplace that hold us back from achieving success.

Many organizations are obsessed with both process and perfection. Those obsessions prevent us from ever feeling like winners.

Over-Processed, Under-Achieved

Process is at every corner in the workplace. It sneaks in everywhere. You know what it is. It's the excruciating, endless talking and hashing and rehashing of every little detail and scenario that could come up in day-to-day operations.

Process…the strategic plans, the pilot studies, and the reviews and revisions. Process…making sure everything is just right. No, better than right…perfect!

It is especially prevalent in education and healthcare because both of those fields have large percentages of women. And, in my opinion, women are much more process-oriented than men. Especially Baby Boomer women like me. I think it's part of how we were raised. We were not raised to go for results. We were steered towards process. Results were almost a bad thing.

When I was a little girl, playing Barbie with my friends was a process. There were no "results" in Barbie. It was a process. We would bring out the cases, show each other the little clothes and tiny (but stylish!) shoes, and if someone didn't have a Barbie bathing suit on the day we were playing beach, we would share one with her. It was most definitely a process, and one that we enjoyed.

At the same time, little boys were involved in team sports. Thank goodness little girls get to play team sports today, but back then, it was just for the boys. So as we were matching up Barbie and Ken for the hundredth time, the boys were playing sports. They were learning the rules and plays and the results that came from them. They also learned, rather early on, that out of all of those things, the most important element was the results—scoring and getting points up on the board.

They also learned that sometimes you have to bend the rules in order to achieve your desired results. For example, in football, it is against the rules to hold, and if you are caught, there is a penalty. But it is an unwritten rule that if holding is what it takes to score, you do it. Now I know some of the women reading this might be gasping, but it is true. The coach knows you are going to hold, the other team knows you are going to hold, your team *hopes* you are going to hold, and even the referee knows you are going to hold. The trick in football is to not get caught!

That is why sometimes men and women struggle when they are on teams together. We girls like process, and the boys prefer results.

One time our senior leadership team went on one of those outside executive retreats. You know the type—climb a rock, feel the grass…blah, blah, blah. I have to tell you I hate being outside…I just do! I know a lot of people enjoy it, but not me. I never have, and as proof of that there is a picture of me when I was about a year old, squatting in the grass, touching it, sobbing away.

I like to look at the outdoors. I just don't like *being* in it. I was born for concrete. In fact, there are a lot of pictures of me sitting on the sidewalk smiling!

Anyway, so here we all are walking through mazes blindfolded and trying to impress our hippie dude facilitator. One of the exercises he had us do was to walk in teams of four on long boards with ropes attached. We were all lined up, with a foot on each board and a rope in each hand. Essentially, they were kind of like giant skis. The goal was to walk about 10 feet up to this rock and turn around and come back. We had to move this board by lifting the ropes (It sounds goofy because it was!), and the deal was that if any member of the team's foot touched the ground, you had to go back and start all over again.

We were split into two teams, and not by design but by coincidence (I promise!), it just so happened that all of the women were on one set of boards and the men were on the other. We started and the ladies did great! We didn't fall off of our boards a single time. We lifted the rope, moved, lifted the rope, moved, etc. We were hoping the hippie dude was dazzled by our brilliant teamwork. *I* was hoping we could finish and go inside.

When we got up to the rock, we voiced our strategy out loud. "Now the team has to operate differently. In order to make these things turn, the people in the front will have to take little narrow steps and the people in the back will take big wide steps," we strategized.

All the while, the men's team was struggling. They hardly took a step without one of them slipping off the boards and touching the ground. They were all talking at once and arguing. Trying to figure out who knew the best way, the fastest way, the most efficient way. Finally, after we ladies were halfway around the rock, the men stepped up to it.

Naturally, we were smirking to ourselves. We thought to ourselves: *These idiots couldn't even walk in a straight line. There is no way they are going to be able to navigate moving around in a circle.* But to our horror, as they stood in front of the rock, the first guy turned around on the boards being very careful not to let his foot touch the grass. The guy behind him got the idea and did the same. The next thing you know they were *all* facing the finish line and heading for it.

We went nuts! We started shouting at the hippie dude, "HEY, HEY! That's not fair! THEY ARE CHEATING!!!"

But to our dismay, the hippie dude did not stop them. Instead he looked at us and said, "What's not fair? I told everyone to go up to the rock, turn around, and come back. You ladies went for process. The gentlemen preferred results!"

The Price of Perfection

There are many circumstances in the workplace where process is appropriate, necessary, and required. Quality improvement is one of those circumstances.

You can't just go trying stuff without a scientific process to back up the change. "Hey, let's try this…Oops! The guy died. Guess it didn't work." But as crazy as that sounds, it can also be crazy to use process in times when it is not only unnecessary, but also a barrier.

One time I was consulting with a customer service committee that was working on first impressions. It was in a hospital so they were focused on things like the switchboard, admitting, security, parking, etc. I suggested to the team that one thing they could try was ordering fresh flowers every week for the information desk. I know that most hospitals have agreements with florists so I didn't think it would be cost prohibitive. So without the expense being a barrier, I knew it would be an easy thing to implement.

But noooooo! I had forgotten I was working with process people. Do you know that someone on the team actually asked me, "Do you have any data that backs up that idea?"

"No! Live on the edge!" I urged them. "Get crazy, woo-hoo! Look at us—we are wild! We are ordering flowers without any data!"

If you are smiling to yourself now, it is because you have worked on teams exactly like that. Groups that immerse themselves in so much process that nothing ever gets done. And that leads to drudgery and negativity.

The other thing that holds us back is the need to be perfect. Oh! We love this one, because it can keep us from ever having to change. Try to implement something new, and you will have people roaring, "Hey! That's not going to work all the time. What about Tuesday mornings or Friday afternoons?!? What about on the days we have meetings?!? What if you are standing on your left foot looking out the east window on a Saturday night when the moon is full?!? It is never going to work then!"

We stall change by waiting for things to be perfect. And it slows us down, then wears us down, and then breaks us down for no reason. Change does not have to be perfect. It just has to be a little bit better.

Postponed Perfection Always Leaves You Wanting More

When is Thanksgiving? (I know I am veering a bit here, but bear with me!) Thanksgiving is always the fourth Thursday in November. And that day is when most of us eat our Thanksgiving dinner. I know some families have different traditions, but the majority of people eat Thanksgiving dinner on that fourth Thursday in November.

But what if healthcare were in charge of it? Oh, then things would be different. First thing we would do is form a giant committee. It would have to be HOUSE-WIDE. We couldn't just have one nurse. No, we would need a nurse from Cardiology, Surgery, Oncology, the ED, Mother-Baby, and so it would go for every division, every department, every job class, every shift.

Oh, and this big committee would then be divided into sub-committees and the work would be endless. Some groups would start working on Pareto charts. There might be a fishbone diagram on side dishes. Should we have okra or green beans, cornbread or sage dressing? Some teams would bring in focus groups and ask, "Should we have a tom turkey or a hen? Fresh or frozen? Is turkey enough? What about the people who don't eat turkey?"

And sometime around November 20th an email would go out to the entire organization. It would read something like this: *Here at Acme Hospital we strive for excellence in all we do. So in keeping with our high standards, we are postponing the implementation of Thanksgiving dinner in order to provide you with a meal that will meet our measure of excellence.*

Ever see an email like that? Sure you have! Maybe not about Thanksgiving, but about something that was supposed to happen but is put off because it is not perfect.

Now, going back to our example, can we have Thanksgiving in December? No, it's already packed with other holidays. Can we have it in January or February? Nope, we are too busy then. So after months of delay, sometime in March the committee would reconvene. Well, about half of them. It will have been so long since Thanksgiving Day passed them by that the other poor souls won't even remember that they never ate. Those at the meeting would set the date for the dinner. And after that "Thanksgiving Day" would roll around with mixed results, they would gather post-meal to debrief. Inevitably, someone on the planning committee would complain, "You know what is wrong about this place? Nobody appreciates anything. We have worked on this meal for over six months, and people didn't even seem to appreciate it."

Maybe that's because it's almost spring!

No matter what, most of us eat Thanksgiving dinner on that fourth Thursday in November. And it is never perfect, is it? Of course not! But if you burn the bottom of the rolls, do you leave the kitchen and announce to everyone, "Sorry, we are going to have to postpone Thanksgiving! The rolls are burnt!" No one does that. If you burn the bottom of the rolls, what do you do? *Cut them off* and move on.

Have you ever served Jell-o with a ladle? You know, it is a cruel myth that anyone can make Jell-o because it just isn't true. I've seen it. Or say the dog jumps in the pie—do you tell everyone, "Well, we almost made it through the whole meal, but we are going to have to do it again tomorrow." Nope! Dog jumps in the pie, you grab some Cool Whip, don't you? Well, at least that's what I do.

The point is, the meal we eat the fourth Thursday in November is rarely perfect, but it is almost always really good. And at the very least, isn't it always better than the meal we eat on the third Thursday in November? I'll say it again. Change doesn't have to be perfect; it just needs to be better.

If we didn't always have to go from black to white, zero to one hundred, we could have less resistance to change and therefore better work environments. Little changes can add up, and they are not as painful.

In order to have great places to work, we need to accomplish things, get results. We can't let process hold us back. And as those results start to happen, we need to be prepared to accept less than perfect change. If we can manage to eliminate both process and perfection paralysis, it will be easier to create a positive workplace.

5

The Power of the Shout-Out: Why Recognition Is Important in the Workplace

A lot has been said about recognition. In fact whole books have been devoted to explaining why its presence is so key when trying to create a positive work environment. Most of us are familiar with the statistic that indicates how many compliments versus criticisms must be handed out in order to foster a positive work environment. But just in case you aren't familiar with it, the ratio is 3:1. That means in order to have a positive work environment, it takes three compliments to correct the negativity that is felt after one criticism.

We have also seen the data telling us how vital recognition is when trying to motivate the younger generations. But, rest assured, shout-outs (though we probably don't call them that) are important for us Baby Boomers too! In fact, we Baby Boomers are a funny group. We claim recognition doesn't matter to us, but it does. We've all worked for bosses who are miserable at recognition, and for the most part, their cluelessness made us miserable.

As I am writing this (on a plane, where else?), my complimentary copy of *USA Today* is next to me. In it is one of their famous "Snapshots." In this particular Snapshot, readers were asked, *What makes good employees quit?* These were the top reasons given:

- Unhappiness with management—35%
- Limited opportunities for advancement—33%
- Lack of recognition—13% **(Hello!)**
- Inadequate salary and benefits—13%
- Being bored—1%

As you can see "Lack of recognition" is tied with "Inadequate salary and benefits." And I am going to go out on a limb and guess that the management teams, which 35 percent of those polled were unhappy with, are probably not so good with the whole recognition deal.

Recognition Is Key, Let Me Count the Ways

So with everything that is already out there about recognition, why do I want to devote a chapter to it? I have a couple of reasons. For starters, despite everything that has been written, spoken, and shared about recognition, a lot of us are still uncomfortable with it. I think I can provide some insight that will change that.

The second reason is that I believe that recognition is not only important to the individuals who are being acknowledged, but it's vital to the entire organization and its culture. And lastly, I think the best way to implement change in an organization is to recognize the behaviors that you would like to see repeated.

In fact, let's start with that last reason.

Years ago I read a book called *Don't Shoot the Dog!: The New Art of Teaching and Training*. To this day it remains one of my favorites on not only training and development, but also on how to create a positive workplace environment. That book is where I first read the quote, "Recognize behaviors that you would like to see repeated." So perfect, so simple!

In fact, I always say that should be every organization's entire recognition plan. No long policy, no special criteria, and no guidelines are necessary. Simply, recognize the behaviors you want to see repeated. It's exquisite, really. It seems so basic that most of us want to disregard it. But I am telling you it is beautiful! And it will help us reach everyone we work with.

Let's say Lauren has been a nurse on your unit for 20 years. She regularly pitches in and works extra when needed. She even comes in on her days off if things are really tight. If that is a behavior you would like good ol' Lauren to repeat, you had better recognize her. You don't have to send flowers; just do something. Say "thank you" next time you see her, send a nice email, or heck, even leave a handwritten thank-you note in her locker. The message could go something like—are you ready?—"Lauren, thanks for covering the shift yesterday!"

See, it's not rocket science. You don't need to read a book, check a policy, or draft a proposal. Just recognize.

It can work in all kinds of ways. Here is another one: Teresa is a tech working in the ED. You have been coaching her since she started a year ago. You are trying to get her to act on her own. You want her to take patients over to the X-Ray Department after she sees that an x-ray has been ordered instead of waiting to be told to do so. (Do you have a Teresa in your department?)

Finally, after 13 months, she does it. She sees the requisition; reads it; finds the patient; checks the ID bracelet; confirms that the requisition, patient, and test all match…and then miracle of miracles, she wheels the patient over to X-Ray. Now, if you ever want Teresa to do that again, you had better recognize her.

It doesn't matter that it has taken 13 months for the employee to follow procedure. It doesn't matter that your team might not see it as a big deal. It doesn't matter that you secretly think it's ridiculous to recognize behavior she should have gotten down pat in the first week (if not the first day). "Wow! Teresa finally found X-Ray after 13 months. Whoopee! Let's have a party for her!"

Nope, none of that matters. The simple truth is that when you recognize Teresa, you are solidifying the new behavior. You are encouraging her to do it again. Recognize behaviors you would like to see repeated—beautiful!

Are you starting to see how key recognition can be if we are working to implement a change, or if we are asking people to adopt new behaviors? Leaders can be great support by recognizing when their staff adopts a new behavior. And recognition works especially well when people are not comfortable with the new behavior being adopted, such as using new keywords or service recovery.

So for example, the first time you hear someone say to a customer, "I am so sorry that happened to you," recognize him. Say, "Hey, Tyler, that was great! I noticed the visitor's face when you told her you were sorry for her inconvenience, and she immediately softened and responded to your words. Thanks for doing that so well! I could tell you were just a touch uncomfortable, but you really made a difference."

Not only is Tyler more likely to repeat that new behavior, but he will likely feel more comfortable the next time he does so. Recognition can play a vital role in solidifying any organizational change.

When It Comes to Recognition…Stick It to 'Em!

And that brings me back to my first reason for including a chapter on recognition in this book. (Yes, I've always done things in an unconventional order; why do you ask?) Giving recognition is a change for most of us, and one we are not all comfortable with. While it may come very naturally for a few people, most of us struggle with it. I think we struggle because despite all that is known about the importance of recognition, in our day-to-day work lives it is still a rare commodity.

There are only a few rules of thumb when it comes to giving recognition in the workplace. You already know the primary one. You know, recognize behaviors you want to see repeated…blah, blah, blah. After that just be genuine, sincere, and specific. Pay attention because these qualities are equally important! You have to be genuine, and by that I mean true to yourself. People have to believe what you are saying/doing is coming from you, not from a manual or an administrative directive.

One time I was helping a surgical department improve their culture, and we were focusing on recognition. The charge nurses and lead techs decided that when someone was to be recognized on their shift or in their team, they would pass out heart stickers or butterfly stickers, I can't remember exactly. But what I do remember is this big guy named Paul taking me aside. He seemed nervous and uneasy as he spoke to me. He said, "Liz, I am totally behind this recognition thing. Especially if it is going to help the team. But I cannot see myself giving anybody a butterfly sticker. It just isn't in me."

Poor Paul! I totally understood where he was coming from. (Hey, I'm not the sappy sticker type either!) And I also knew that if Paul was passing out hearts and flowers, the team was just not going to buy it. I told Paul to take a couple of days to think about what would work for him. The following week I received a great email from Paul telling me that he found Bob the Builder stickers. He started passing those out to convey, as he put it, "Ya know, building a great team together!"

My point is that Paul met the recognition requirements. He just put his own spin on it. He was sincere in his desire to recognize his team; he was very specific about what behaviors (teamwork) he was recognizing; and he found a very genuine way to accomplish it. He made it his own!

Recognize for the Right Reasons

Now let's talk about the importance of recognition within the organization. We have known for a long time that recognition is important to individuals. But I believe we have failed to realize how very vital it is to organizational culture.

Recognition defines us. It tells our teams what we value and what is truly important to us. It is not unusual for organizations to lay out visions and values. But unless individuals are recognized for living those values, they are just etchings in a plaque on the wall.

And when we are performing recognition, it is essential that everyone in the organization knows who is getting acknowledged and why. Quint Studer calls it "connecting the dots." I believe it is essential for creating pride in our work, which brings us back to the positive work environment.

A few years back, I had a one-year engagement with a hospital. The organization decided that one of the themes they wanted to embrace while I was with them was teamwork. One of the strategies they employed was to honor a team each month who had provided great service. In the past, they had selected an employee of the month. However, in order to encourage teamwork, that particular year would be different. They would, instead, recognize a team. It didn't need to be a formal team or committee, but it would always be more than one person.

The first team honored consisted of two techs and a nurse from Ambulatory Surgery. Here's why they were recognized: One day, a woman came in from a residential facility for mentally handicapped adults. She was having a quick, simple procedure and was going to return to the facility when it was done. The entire time she was in pre-op she was crying and asking for her doll. Apparently, she had a doll that served as a sort of security blanket for her. In fact, it was so important that the people who cared for her at the facility didn't send it to the hospital with her because they feared it could get lost.

Unfortunately, without the doll the woman was inconsolable. So when she went for her procedure, the two techs and the nurse went to the supply room and got some Ace bandages, Kerlix, and Kling. Kerlix and Kling are white, fluffy bandages. And if you don't know what an Ace bandage is, I can't help you.

Anyway, they took all the bandages and made the woman a rag doll so that she would have something to hold when she came out of surgery. And that is why they were the first team to be recognized by the hospital.

The hospital leaders wanted to make a big deal out of this so they had the presentation at noon in the cafeteria, the time of day when the largest number of employees would be able to witness the event. The leaders were confident it would be a big hit with everyone….

Yep, you guessed it—there is a "but" in there. *But* it wasn't the grand slam they had all hoped for. Some people in the organization were mad. Staff from Purchasing complained, "We have to watch every nickel and dime we spend, and this bunch gets rewarded for wasting supplies?!?"

The Med-Surg nurses were not happy either, "We haven't been off of this unit to eat lunch in over two weeks, and they are doing *arts and crafts* and getting recognized for it?!?" (Ugh! Don't you get SO TIRED of whiners, complainers, and naysayers?)

Oh, the leadership team was devastated as they met after the celebration! They began second-guessing themselves, "Maybe we should have put in better criteria," "Maybe we should consider ROI," or "Maybe we should revise our guidelines."

"Don't you dare!" I responded. I explained to them that they had recognized the right people for the right reasons. And in doing so they had sent a strong message to their organization. The woman they helped was never going to fill out a patient satisfaction survey. She was never going to go to a cocktail party and recommend the hospital. But in recognizing those three individuals, they sent a loud message to the entire organization: "THIS IS WHO WE ARE, AND THIS IS WHAT WE BELIEVE IN!"

And even though not everybody in the audience had been on board that afternoon, I bet them that at least 25 percent of those who had been in the cafeteria were moved, motivated, and, most importantly, proud of what their colleagues had done. And I told them that the next month that number would go up to 40 percent and so on and so on.

You see, this is how we restore pride in our workplaces. This is how we move people from thinking about their job as a way to earn a paycheck to remembering that they are doing something special, something real, something meaningful. This is how we turn negative work environments into positive ones—by focusing on what is right, what is good, and what we take pride in!

6

Infinitely Grateful: Lessons in Workplace Gratitude

People who work in positive workplaces display gratitude and graciousness. It might be a hard thing to pinpoint at first. Sometimes people say things like, "This place seems different," or, "There is a really good vibe here." That good vibe is gratitude!

On the other hand, when gratitude and graciousness are missing, it is just as evident. Often the people in those environments are described as having a sense of entitlement. Those who come into contact with them might say, "There is just no pleasing those people!"

"Thanks!": The Proper Complement to Compliments

Now as you read this, you might be thinking about your boss or administration as you nod your head. *That's right*, you're thinking. *My boss never appreciates anything*. But that was covered in Chapter 5. This one is about all of us becoming more gracious and being genuinely thankful for the things we have or receive.

I understand that you might be a little nervous or suspicious about a boss, who in the past had never said anything good, but then all of a sudden after attending a seminar, he starts doling out compliments left and right. And it is even more difficult to give out a lot of recognition when it is never received with grace.

But let's look at it for a moment from the boss's side. He goes to a conference. He's told that if he really wants to make an impact on his team he should recognize them for the great work they do. It feels a little awkward to him and the rest of the leaders at the seminar, but they commit to giving it a try.

The first person this boss compliments is a team member who has been working in the department for a long, long time. The boss approaches her and says, "Hi, Lucy. I just want to tell you that I really appreciate all that you do for this department. You are a valued member of the team."

Lucy responds by looking somewhat surprised and uncomfortable. Unsure of how to respond, she just lowers her eyes and mutters, "Whatever" as she walks away.

Hmmm, this is not the response the boss was hoping for. So he tries again. He goes up to another team member and tries even harder. "Hey, Tom! The way you handled that family was fantastic. I could tell you went out of your way, and it really made a difference to them."

Tom looks up and says, "Oh, it was nothing," and walks away. How much longer do you think that boss is going to want to walk around recognizing people? Do you think that if Lucy or Tom had said even just a brief "thanks" it would have made a difference?

Now, I don't know if you call that graciousness or gratitude, but it really doesn't matter. We can't expect people to appreciate us if we don't receive their compliments with thankfulness.

We need to do this as individuals and as teams. When the organization does something in an attempt at recognition, everyone needs to appreciate the effort. Otherwise the recognition will go away.

A Failure in Graciousness

Take this story from my experience as a hospital administrator. Allow me to set the stage: I was a new VP. Everyone was working hard. It was busy. It was January. And I met with Quint and told him that I wanted to do something really nice for the staff because they had been working really hard.

He asked me what I was thinking and I said, "Let's do pizza and pop. (I'm from the Midwest, so, yes, I say pop!) And I'm thinking about how I want to do it...Let's do it on a Sunday, a Monday, and a Tuesday. That way, the weekend people could be first for once instead of always being last."

He thought it was a good idea, so I started planning it. This was to be my first time arranging something for the entire hospital, and, naturally, I wanted it to go very well. So as I'm planning, I'm trying to figure out my pizza formula. What kinds of pizza should I order to make sure everyone's happy? Some people don't eat meat. Some people don't eat dairy. Some people don't eat this, some people don't eat that. Make sure we have this kind, that kind... blah, blah, blah. I kind of feel if you don't eat cheese and you don't eat sausage, then just don't eat pizza, but that's my own opinion!

So, Sunday comes and the pizza plan is in effect. Then on Monday I start walking around. I'm thinking that people are going to start embracing me with open arms, "Oh, Liz, you are the nicest, bestest administrator EVER!"

The first floor I walked onto I asked, "So, what do you think about the pizzas?" And they snapped at me! More or less their sentiment was something like this, "Oh, it's real nice! You know, we haven't gotten to eat lunch in the last two weeks, but does anyone notice? Noooo! And now the pizzas are down in the cafeteria and we can't get to them. But people who aren't taking care of patients, like the business office and IT, they are all down there eating pizza while we're up here working!"

Wow, I wasn't expecting that. I think there might have even been some foot stomping or chart flinging involved.

I was devastated. I had tried so hard to get it right, and my intentions were noble. I mean it is not like I went to Quint's office and said, "You know, everybody's really working hard. Might be a really fun time to mess with them."

Quint: "What do you want to do? Turn off the hot water?"

Me: "Nah, we did that last year."

Quint: "Mess with the computers?"

Me: "I don't think so. I got it! Let's order a whole bunch of pizzas and make sure no one has time to go down to the cafeteria to eat them. Then we can tease them even more by pointing the fans in the cafeteria at the ventilation system so that the smell of delicious pizza wafts through the entire place."

Quint: "And maybe we can get the guys from IT or the ladies from the business office to go up to some of the floors with plates full of pizza and say, 'Look what we're doing! We're eating great pizza! Ha ha ha, you can't have any!'"

Graciousness is not hard. All you need to do is offer a simple "thanks." And if there is a problem, you can add, "That was a great idea, Liz, but (fill in your problem here)."

Now, I did learn from that experience. I knew that the next time I should have the pizzas delivered directly to the units. But had I been someone with a different personality, I might have just decided never to order pizzas (or do anything else special) ever again.

Thank You for Putting Your Trust in Us Today

If you are unaccustomed to getting compliments, it may take some time for you to feel comfortable receiving them. Just practice and be prepared for some kind words! When I first started speaking, I had no idea what to say to people when they told me they liked my presentation. I had to rehearse being gracious and grateful. Can you imagine if someone came up to me and said, "I just loved your speech!" and I responded with, "Whatever"? Yikes and double yikes! It seems so funny we should have to practice saying "thank you."

Once we have mastered the gratitude thing with our bosses and each other, we need to move on to the people we serve. Something that can be very tough in education or healthcare. When I first told my staff that we ought to be thanking our patients, one of them replied, "What are we supposed to say? 'Thank you for breaking your leg'?"

Obviously not. My suggestion was that they say, "Thank you for putting your trust in us today."

One day shortly after that talk with my team, I was walking through the department, and I heard one of our best nurses speaking to an older gentleman. Now the man had come from a long-term care facility and was not awake or alert. He was in the end stages of Alzheimer's. He was not aware of his surroundings or circumstance.

As I moved closer, I heard Eileen, the nurse, say to him, "Mr. Murphy, we are going to call the ambulance to take you back to your facility. I just want to say thank you for putting your trust in us today."

I kind of shook my head in disbelief, and when Eileen walked out of the room, I pulled her over to the side. "Eileen, I know I said that we had to start saying thank you to people, but if they are unconscious or can't hear you and don't know where they are, you don't have to say it," I clarified.

"I know that, Liz," she replied, slightly irritated.

"Well, I don't know that you do," I continued. "I just heard you in the room with that gentleman. He clearly didn't know what was going on and you thanked him."

"I was practicing," she answered and walked away.

No wonder Eileen was one of the best. She knew it would be difficult to start thanking our patients, so first she tried it out on some people who wouldn't mind.

I know that the best places to work are places where teams are grateful for what is given to them and aren't afraid to express sincere appreciation whenever it is merited. The best places to work are those where individuals accept compliments and praise with grace and don't second-guess the intention.

We already have a lot to be grateful for every day. And if we work on both team and individual gratitude and graciousness, our work environment will be even healthier, and you will see negativity slip away.

7

Judge Not, Lest Ye Be Bugged: How Judging Hurts You and Leads to Burnout

Judging is one of my favorite subjects. Why? Probably because I used to be so good at it. But judging is the enemy of any positive workplace. It is by far one of the most self-destructive things we do. And most importantly, in healthcare, judging is the number one cause of burnout.

Judging is when we let certain things that our patients or customers do bug us so much that our annoyance builds and ruins our day. Judging affects the quality of our work life. And it affects our ability to enjoy our work and feel good about what we are doing.

Now, it's normal to have a few things that bug you. In fact, when you are new to your job, specialty, or department, you almost certainly have a short list of things—normal, rational things—that bug you.

For example, let's say you are working in Purchasing and someone calls you in a tizzy. "We need a such-and-such kit up here right away!" she demands. "Someone used the last one and forgot to order a replacement! Dr. Snip is on his way up here, and it is the only kind he'll use!"

"What's the order number?" you ask.

"I don't know the order number. It is a BLUE BOX, with yellow letters on it somewhere!" the caller screams. "Or maybe they are white. OH, JUST SEND IT!!!"

If you work in Purchasing, a call like that is going to bother you. Of course it is. And that is okay, because it is normal. If that pet peeve is just one of a few things on a short list, then you don't have a problem.

The problem occurs when the list of stuff that bugs you gets to be too long. That is what causes burnout. It is not that we are old or tired. It is that our list gets to be too long. When you are new to healthcare, the list is short. If you have only three or four things on your list, you can work three or four days without being bothered.

But the longer you are working in healthcare, the longer the list tends to get.

After 18 years of working in hospital EDs, I probably had about 120 things on my "things that bug me" list! And when the list gets that long, you are constantly annoyed.

Shoe-Heel Smashers, Pants Unzippers, and You

I had some of the craziest things on my list! I used to get bugged by people who would smash down the backs of their shoes. Do you know what I mean? Basically, they would make their own pair of scuff slippers. I guess they didn't know how to buy the right size sneaker, so they would just smash down the back. They would come into my ED, all bent over and shuffling in their shoes with the smashed down backs. "I'm sick. I'm sick," they would moan. And I would think, "All right, you're sick! Were you too sick to put your shoes on all the way?"

Man, that used to bug me! But at the end of the day, despite what I thought at the time, the loser in that situation was me, not the guy with the smashed shoes! It's not like he planned it. I mean, how would that go exactly? A buddy asks him, "Hey! You going to the ED later?" He says, "Yeah, I was thinking about it." And then his buddy says, "Cool. Wanna have a little fun? Smash down the backs of your shoes. It really makes them crazy over there!"

So what I'm saying is that, really, *I* was the nut in the shoe-heel situation. And it didn't stop there. (I told you I had a lot on my list!) Another thing that really bothered me was people coming in with their pants unzipped because of their stomach pain. They want everyone in the Emergency Department to know their pain is worse than everyone else's. To prove it, they come in with their pants unzipped.

Have you ever seen that? It's not pretty! They walk in with their pants wide open saying, "Oh, my belly hurts. My belly hurts!" All right, we get it. Now zip that up because you're making *my* belly hurt, not to mention what you're doing to my eyes and head.

Now, let's say it's just an average work day for me in the Emergency Department. First some guy comes in with his shoes all smashed down. Immediately, I'm aggravated with him! Twenty or thirty minutes pass and some woman walks in with her pants wide open. Now, I'm aggravated with her! I'm not going to have a good day, am I? If you are aggravated two or three times an hour, you are never going to have a good day.

Judging Hurts the Judger

Judging hurts us! It's self-destructive. That's the main reason I talk about it in every one of my staff presentations. I know we've been taught our whole lives not to judge. We're taught it in school. "Don't judge." We're taught it at church. "Judge not, lest ye be judged." And they tried to teach me that at the hospital. They said, "Liz, don't be so judgmental. You need to put yourself in the patients' shoes for a change." And I said, "If I did, they'd at least be on all the way!"

Let me say it again: Judging hurts us. It hurts *us*. It doesn't hurt the customers or patients; it hurts *us*. We are the ones in a bad mood at work every day. We are the ones aggravated 2-3 times an hour.

If you can't make a difference, you have to learn to let it go. Even when your reasons for being upset are rational, if you can't make a difference, then you still have to let it go!

Now I want to share with you a nurse/patient scenario I use when I am presenting. I tell this story and I always ask the audience the same questions. For the 12 years I have been doing it, my audiences have always given me the same answers. First, I ask that you put yourself in the nurse's shoes (Make sure they're on all the way!) and really think about how you would react in this situation. (Be honest!) While my story is about one patient, she does three things that are going to bug the nurse about her. She's like a little trifecta of aggravation. Okay, here goes:

A mom walks into the Emergency Department triage with an 18-month-old baby:
   Mom: "My baby has a fever."

What do you think will bug the nurse first? What would bug you if you were in her position? If you guessed that the mom doesn't know what the temperature is, you guessed correctly! That exchange usually goes like this:
   Nurse: "Really? Your baby has a fever? What's the baby's temperature?"

   Mom: "Oh, I don't know. I don't have a thermometer. I just felt her."

   Nurse (muttering under her breath): "Oh, you're a scientist, are you?"

Okay, let me interrupt here to tell you a story about something that happened to me during my clinical days. I think you'll find that it proves just how frighteningly realistic my nurse anecdote really is.

One day when I was working in the ED, a woman came in and said to me, "My baby has a fever."

I said, "Really? What is it?"

She said, "It's 350."

"Three fifty?" I said. "Well then, it's come down nicely, hasn't it?"

My sarcasm was lost on the woman. She went on to explain: "Well, I don't have a thermometer, so I put the baby on the kitchen table and I turned on the oven. Then I put one hand on the baby and one hand in the oven." (Do you see where this is going?) "And when the oven got to 350," she continued, "they both felt the same."

I swear, you can't make this stuff up! People are nuts!

Now, back to our original scenario. Our hypothetical mom thinks her baby has a fever, but she hasn't actually checked it with a thermometer. What's the next thing that's going to bug the nurse? That's right. The mom didn't give the baby any medicine to bring the fever down.

   Nurse: "When's the last time the baby had some medicine? Any Motrin? Maybe some Tylenol?"

Usually, at this point, they look at you like puppies with their heads cocked.

   Mom: "What? Give the baby medicine? For a fever? I never thought of that."

   Nurse: "Huh!"

Okay, the third annoying thing occurs when the mom gets her identification out of her purse. It's not that she didn't have insurance or know her pediatrician's name. No, when she opens her purse, the nurse leans over, sneaks a peek, and what does she see? Cigarettes! Yep, now she's mad! And if the woman dumped out her purse, the nurse would see something else that bugs her! What could it be? Think back. We've all been there. Right behind the cigarettes is a new, state-of-the-art cell phone! And, if that mother has artificial fingernails…Wow, that nurse will really be mad!

It All Comes Down to the Missing Screen!

The nurse in the scenario probably assumed this woman was programmed like her. Now, of course, she knows everyone is different and unique in their own way. But, basic human programming should be about the same. Or let's say humans are like computer programs, essentially just a series of screens. And if we're all basically programmed alike, there should be a very basic screen that reads:

If you are a decent parent, before you spend money on cigarettes, buy a thermometer and keep some Tylenol in your house!

Right? A very basic screen for most, but this particular mother is missing that screen.

We can flip through her program 100 times and never find the "prioritize your spending" screen—simply because it does not exist. And because she doesn't have the screen, she doesn't understand why the nurse is upset with her. All she sees is someone who is unfriendly.

I had to beg my ED staff for one month not to get mad at mothers who don't check their child's temperature (There are a lot of them!) before bringing them into the ED. Judging hurts you! It makes life harder for you. If you can't make a difference in certain situations, you have to learn to let them go.

In our Maternal/Child Unit, we thought we could wipe out teenage pregnancy on the South Side of Chicago by rolling our eyes! ("You're how old?" *Eye roll.*) Obviously, that approach didn't work. If it did, we would have published it! If you're working in Maternal/Child and you think you will never see a pregnant teenager, you're delusional. Again, if you can't make a difference, you have to learn to let it go.

If you work in Purchasing and you don't like the nursing units, you are never going to have a good day. If you work in the Operating Room and don't like the surgeons, you're going to have a problem. If you don't like the patients, you can't like the job. If you don't like the customers, you can't like the job. If you work in the Billing Department and don't like insurance companies, don't even bother getting out of the car. That sounds so simple, doesn't it? But it can be very difficult to keep in mind when you're racing through yet another chaotic day filled with irritating people.

I used to say, "Wait a minute. I love my patients. Except for people who smash down their shoes, people who don't zip up their pants, and mothers who don't give their babies Tylenol. If only we'd get some decent patients in this hospital, I would love my work!"

Unfortunately for me—and for you—the hospital with the perfect clientele does not exist. If you have a long list of things that bother you, you will never ever have a good day. You are in control of the way you feel about your job. If your list is too long, you are the only one who can change that.

At the start of this book, I said that we feel great about our work when we make a difference. The reverse is true as well. When we can't make a difference, it tires us, it drags us down, it burns us out. If you can't make a difference, you have to learn to let it go.

My staff went along with me when I asked them not to get mad at those moms. It wasn't easy, but guess what? At the end of the month, the workplace was less negative. There was a small but noticeable improvement, and the biggest winners were the ED staff themselves.

8

Eliminating the Debbie Downers: How Managing Morale Will Help You Create a Great Workplace

Morale. It's what's for dinner. Seriously, it's an important subject. In fact, it's the reason this book on creating positive workplaces ever got started. Here's why: I have been working in healthcare for over 25 years, and I love it. And I love the people working in all areas of healthcare. When I first started writing this book, I thought, and I think everyone else thought, it would be about patient satisfaction or customer service. But a lot of people have already covered those very important topics. So, I kept asking myself, *What do people in healthcare* NEED? The answer was always the same. We need and deserve to have great places to work. And part of achieving that is learning how to manage our own morale...because if I have learned anything these past 30 years, it's that when you leave your morale in someone else's hands, you are destined to be unhappy and dissatisfied.

The bottom line is that in order to create great places to work, we have to address the issue of morale. It's the starting point for everything else.

I became a leader almost 30 years ago. And I've been hearing about morale ever since. People in healthcare love to talk about morale. Sometimes they sound like Chicken Little, "Morale is falling! Morale is falling!" Sometimes they sound like a doomsday news reporter, "Morale is at an all time low!" And sometimes they even sound like thugs, "Morale is in the toilet!"

Morale Is an Inside Job

I believe organizations have certain obligations when it comes to morale. They should create company cultures in which people can manage their own morale. If staff members don't have the skills to do so, then I believe the organization has a responsibility to help them acquire those skills. But most importantly, I believe leaders have to start holding people accountable for their morale.

Truthfully, morale is not the job of the boss. It can't be. In fact, I don't know where we ever came up with the cockamamie theory that the boss is in charge of everyone's morale. One person in charge of making sure *everyone* is happy, *everyone* is in a good mood? It's just crazy! Just think about it. My boss would have had to stand out in the parking lot all day long telling people as they came in, "Put your shoes on all the way! Liz is working!" Or, "Don't even think about walking in there with your pants wide open! Liz is at the desk!"

Individuals are in charge of the way they feel about their jobs. We control our own morale. You control yours. I control mine. As I said in the chapter on judging, if we allow 100 things to bug us, we can't ever have a good day.

We get as much negativity in our departments as we are willing to accept. And I believe that in healthcare, from top to bottom, we are far too accepting of negativity in the workplace. I don't think it is okay for some staff members to come into work every day in a bad mood just because the work is hard. After all, we all know people who come to work every day in a good mood, and they perform the same tough job as those miserable people.

We have to take action to drive negativity out of the workplace. Most of us spend over 2,000 hours at work every year. That is way too much time to be spending in a negative environment. No one deserves that—not even the people who are creating the misery.

One night at an ED staff meeting, I told my staff that our department was becoming way too negative. I asked them, "What can we do to make this ED less negative?" And I didn't have to wait long for their responses:

"Administration ought to change…blah, blah, blah."
"Housekeeping should…blah, blah, blah."
"Security ought to…blah, blah, blah."

I stopped them at every suggestion. Then, I re-asked the question, "What can *WE* do to make this ED less negative?" Asked that way, it was a much tougher question for them to answer. When we are at work and are asked what can be done to make things better, we never start with ourselves. It is always that this guy could do that or that lady could do that or if that other department could…. (You get the picture.)

It was tough that night for us to come up with something *we* could do. The group thought for a long time. But just before the hour was over they came up with the first initiative. It was a small one, but it was a start in the right direction. They decided that in order to make the department less negative they were going to stop saying something to the incoming shifts that had become routine. You know what had become their daily mantra? It was something along the lines of, "Run away! Don't even swipe in! I'll pretend I never saw you! Run for your life!"

Now, it was never said out of malice. In fact it was done in a sense of camaraderie, but it was negative, wasn't it? You bet! I mean what would you think if you were coming in for an 8- or 12-hour shift and your coworkers were yelling, "RUN! FLEE!"? You probably wouldn't start thinking to yourself, "YIPPEE! Another day in paradise for me!"

I was proud of them that night. That one goal started us on a very positive journey. We didn't turn that ED from very negative to positive over night—in fact, it took about three years—but that was the first step. And it worked!

I will tell you that helping my team improve their morale is one of the most fulfilling things that I have done as a leader. Creating a positive workplace is worth every effort you put into it.

Give Negativity the Cold Shoulder

I don't think that most people are negative. But I do believe that too many of us support negativity. The negative person comes into work, throws her pen across the desk, and cries, "This place is crazy!" Most of us mutter something like, "Yeah, I hear you!" Or, "You can sure say that again!" Or some of us just babble, "Yep, yep, yep," while nodding our heads. We shouldn't do that, because the negative person sees that as positive reinforcement. And if someone hears that yep, yep, yep from at least one colleague, day after day, month after month, years go by and the negative person begins to believe that not only is her behavior appropriate, but she thinks her colleagues and superiors actually appreciate it.

Don't do that anymore! One of the most effective ways to let negative people know you don't appreciate their complaints is to ignore them. Say nothing. Let their moans and groans fall on deaf ears. That way they cannot misinterpret our uh-uhs and yep-yeps as positive reinforcement.

We have to save our positive reinforcement for the positive people. Those are the people we need to support.

Shut Up and Eat THAT Cookie!

I was working on morale with a very large—over 200 team members—Mother-Baby division. I helped them implement their first initiative aimed at driving negativity out of the workplace. They decided to declare one day a week No Negativity Day. Just one day, mind you. They thought all seven would be too much, at least at first. Kind of like quitting something cold turkey. But they knew they would be able to handle it for just one day. Maybe it would become a novelty.

Now, the Mother-Baby unit was a 24/7 operation, but no matter who you are or what days you work, Monday is never a good day to have to keep your negativity on lockdown. (Does anybody *really* like Mondays?) So, they picked Tuesday as their "No Negativity Day."

And in order to remind everyone of the "No Negativity" initiative, every Tuesday in the division every department and every shift received a great big tray of sugar cookies with giant yellow smiley faces on them.

And you can be sure there were some negative people in that division who looked at those cookies and said, "This insults me professionally. What am I, some kind of dog? You are going to shove a cookie in my mouth, pat me on the head, and woof, woof, all of a sudden I am in a good mood?!?"

Now, someone might have been standing nearby and when they heard that tirade, they might have added, somewhat innocently, "Yeah, I hear you. You can sure say that again! Yep, yep, yep!"

But you can't and shouldn't do that because the cookies are not the problem, are they? I know that cookies can't solve our problems. I get that. Believe me, I am not that far gone yet. But I also know that cookies are not the problem, are they? *Cookies? A problem?* Never, ever, ever!

No, cookies aren't the problem. The problem is the person standing in front of you complaining, the one who complains about everything. You get a blue tote bag for hospital week and she whines about that. "Why is it blue?" she asks. "Why can't we ever pick out our own color? Maybe just once a green or yellow one. And why is it always a tote bag? How many tote bags can a person use in their lifetime? I wish they would just put that money in my check."

"All right! Here is your four bucks. Feeling better?" is how I always wanted to respond to whiners like that.

Your focus should be with the people who bring in smiley face cookies trying to make the place better. Those are the people you support. And if you have a negative person saying, "We have work coming out of our ears, but it's Happy Tuesday, so I guess I'd better pretend to be in a good mood," instead of saying "Yep, yep, yep," it is time to turn to those negative types and say, "**Shut up and eat THAT cookie!**"

Working in healthcare is way too hard a job to have to also be putting up with people who are in a bad mood every day. We owe it to ourselves to manage our own and our team's morale.

Healthcare is not going to get any easier. We can't be working with people who put us and the rest of our team on eggshells every day. We have to let them know it is not okay.

We need to create positive work environments, because it will make a huge difference in the way our units or departments run. Think about this. Say you are working one day, and you get to work and find out two people have called in sick. You are short clerical support and the census is off the wall. But you take one look at the team members working with you that day and you see that all of the people on duty are positive. Then things don't seem quite so bad after all. You think to yourself, *We are going to be just fine today no matter what.*

But then there are other days when you are fully staffed and the census is bearable, but you look at the schedule and see the people working with you for the day. It is full of negative people, and you think to yourself, *This is going to be a really long day.*

We can't have those kinds of days anymore. We need to make sure that we create positive workplaces. Doing so will give us the strength we need to face difficult times and still feel great about our work!

9

Lessons in the F-Word: How to Make Your Workplace "FUN"!

When creating positive workplaces, I have three rules about fun. It should be planned, protected, and mandatory. Yep, I said it, MANDATORY! I truly believe that fun in the workplace needs to be mandatory. I mean, think about it. Fun people don't need fun. That is why we call them fun—because they already are. "Oh, that Cathy, she is a blast…what a fun girl!" But there are bound to be people on your team who aren't fun. For example, people like Mary, "Eww, Mary, she is such a drag!" Which girl do you think needs the mandatory fun? Cathy? Of course not. She is *already* fun. It is Mary who needs the fun. Even if you have to pull her kicking and screaming, drag her as she cries, "I don't want to have fun!" Tell her, "YOU WILL HAVE FUN!" C'mon just pull her along. Yep, that's mandatory fun.

The planned and protected rules are also important. Because we are all so busy if we don't *plan* for fun, it will never happen. And leaders need to *protect* fun because there will always be those individuals who think it is frivolous, a waste of time, or beneath them. Some of those people might be your superiors. You need to remind them that fun is a form of communication. It breaks down barriers, strengthens teams, and assists with change management.

Every year *Fortune* magazine publishes a list of the 100 best companies to work for. The companies on the list vary from very big to very small. They vary from manufacturing to services to IT and even healthcare. They are from all parts of the country and are very different from one another. But they each always have one thing in common. One of the ways the people who work for these companies describe their workplaces is "fun"!

Hokey Does the Trick

All of us spend a lot of time at work, and as such, we need to have fun workplaces. I am not saying they have to be like playgrounds or country clubs. I am suggesting we set aside four or five minutes a day to lighten up.

> Sure, we do very serious work. But that doesn't mean we have to take ourselves seriously 24/7. There is a Scottish quote that says, "The angels can fly because they take themselves lightly." And I think that sentiment should be applied to those working in healthcare.

For work time fun, I've found that the thing to strive for is hokey. Trust me, hokey works. Now, it took me a while to find this out. I am not naturally hokey. I am an ED nurse, and as such, I prefer that dark, sick, sarcastic kind of humor. And I am really good at it. But that kind of fun is not appropriate in the workplace. Hokey works better. Just taking a few minutes to recharge, laugh at ourselves, relax. Are smiley face cookies hokey? Oh yeah, you bet! But if looking at the goofy cookie before you eat it helps you lighten up for 4-5 minutes, then the humble cookie has done its job.

Now, let's put things in perspective for a second. When I am talking about fun, I am not talking about the most fun you have ever had. It is work, remember! You and your team will probably not be going around saying, "Wowee! We had cookies at work! Yipppee! Best. Day. Ever." Come to think of it, that reaction might be more pathetic than fun. Fun, in this environment, means taking just 4-5 minutes to take yourself less seriously.

Pictures, They're Worth 1,000 Laughs

It is hard to give prescriptions for fun, because they really need to be decided by your teams. But I can give you some suggestions. If you are not used to creating fun in your workplace, try starting with pictures. Baby picture contests are fun. Again, probably not the most fun you have ever had in your life, but amusing nonetheless. And all staff members have to do is bring in baby pictures of themselves.

One goofy hospital I worked with told me, "We tried that baby picture contest. It didn't work!"

It didn't work? I thought to myself. *How could that be?*

"What happened?" I asked.

"Only one person brought in their picture," a staff member said.

"Well, did you hang it up?" I asked. "Because most of the time, if you hang up the first one, other people see it and then they bring in theirs."

"It was past the deadline!" she humphed.

Insert giant eye roll from me! Clearly, this woman didn't get it. Now do you see why we need mandatory fun?

I love using pictures to create fun, and I don't think they need to be confined to baby picture contests. One of the most fun things I think you can do with pictures is to ask people to bring in their prom pictures. And it's really great to do it in the spring around prom time.

When I am speaking, I ask my audiences who went to their prom in the mid-'70s. For those youngsters who might be reading this, let me explain something about formal wear in the '70s. Girls' dresses were usually made out of one of two kinds of material. The good girls wore Gunne Sax—you know, those dresses that made us look like a character out of *Little House on the Prairie*. They were made of eyelet lace and were usually cream or pastel in color. The not-so-good girls wore qiana. Qiana was a polyester fabric so synthetic that if you got it too close to an iron, cigarette, or even a car heater, it didn't burn, it melted…dissolved really. You would be amused at how many women in my audience admit to wearing the qiana. Oh, and they laugh as they raise their hands, not because they are admitting being a touch wild in high school, but because just the thought of those dresses brings them 4-5 minutes of fun.

Now, we can't leave out the men! During the '70s the boys were wearing Easter egg colored tuxedos. You know the ones with the wide lapels, ruffled shirts, and giant bow ties. I have had executives in my audiences admit to wearing tuxedos that were powder blue, lavender, and even yellow plaid. Now that is fun!

Yep, pictures usually work out great. You can try to do wedding pictures, but sometimes they go up with a half missing. People love to bring in pictures of their children and families doing special things. And, oh, their pets! People love, love, love to bring in pictures of their pets.

I must admit, I get into the pet pictures too. I have a little dog named Elvis. Now I am not a big Elvis fan; I just always thought it was a funny name for a dog. That is until the day he got out of the yard. Yep, you guessed it. I had to walk through my neighborhood for over an hour yelling, "Elvis! Elvis! Where are you, Elvis? Come here! C'mon Elvis, where are you?" After a while, one of my neighbors shouted out his front window, "Lady, he's dead!"

Time to Cheer Up

If you are working in an organization that is not used to having fun, it takes a while for everyone to get on board. One day I was sitting with the nurse leader of another unit at the hospital where I was working. A nurse from my unit approached us. She asked if it would be okay if the staff wore Easter bonnets on Easter Sunday. I said sure, that would be okay. The other leader was horrified, "That is the most unprofessional thing I have ever heard of!"

"Oh, don't worry," I said, as I sensed her concern. "Only the women will wear them."

She was still not convinced, so I went on to explain, "Listen, I have a very tight screening process when I hire new people on this unit. One of the questions I ask them is, 'If you are wearing a goofy hat and a code is called, do you A) tighten the chin strap and rush on in, B) run the other way and pretend you didn't hear the code, or C) take off the hat, and go to the code?' If you have people working for you who don't know enough to take off a goofy hat during a serious situation, you have a lot more than a fun problem."

At Holy Cross, we had to cheer. I am not kidding. At every staff meeting, gathering, or hospital event, we had to cheer. I will never forget the first time I told my ED staff about the cheer. We were at a meeting one night and I told them, "At the end of the meeting, we are going to do the new Holy Cross cheer."

"You're funny; that's why we like you, Liz," one of them quipped.

"No, I mean it," I replied.

"We're being nice to the patients. Is that not enough for you?" another nurse whined.

Hey, I was under martial law! What could I do? Remember that 90-day period when I was almost fired? I was convinced that the room was bugged or that someone was spying outside.

"We ARE doing that cheer!" I commanded.

"How do you expect me to come to work tomorrow and look anyone in the face if you make me do a goofy cheer here today?" one last nurse whined.

We were in a room with a long rectangular table. So being considerate of their needs, I told them they could stand up and face the walls so they didn't have to look at each other while doing this embarrassing act.

At Holy Cross, we called our employees "partners" and our values spelled out "serve." And so the dreaded cheer began…"Hey! Holy Cross Partners, how do you feel?!?"

And they answered me in the tiniest whisper of a grunt, *"Great. We feel great. Really, really great. S.E.R.V.E."* Oh, and then they all ran out of that room as fast as they could. They wouldn't even look at each other. Some of them even kind of gave a shiver as they exited the meeting room.

Four days later my phone rang, and as I picked it up, I heard about eight extensions click in. And then I heard all eight of them ask in unison, "Hey! Liz Jazwiec, how do you feel?!?"

Oh, and I answered them, "GREAT! I FEEL GREAT! REALLY, REALLY GREAT! S.E.R.V.E.!"

Now, do you think hokey worked that day? I think so. I think they had fun. Do you think they had 4-5 minutes of fun *before* they called me? You bet they did. See, hokey works.

You cannot have a positive workplace without fun. You cannot lead an effective team without fun. Fun lightens us up. It breaks down barriers. It makes us more creative, more open to change, and it improves our resilience.

Now, go on! Get out there, and have some fun! And, remember, make it mandatory!

10

If This Unit Is A-Rockin'...: Why Workplace Celebrations Are Important

There's no denying how hard people in healthcare work every day. We accomplish many things. But when was the last time you celebrated these accomplishments at work? The reality is that our accomplishments are hardly ever celebrated. If we want our organizations to be great places to work, we need to celebrate more. Don't you think?

Celebrations are a very important part of our lives. They are important to us as children and as adults. They help us mark milestones, share our successes, and feel good about reaching life's little dreams and aspirations. They help remind us that not only do struggles and hard work pay off, but when we do reach our goals, they are even sweeter when shared with others.

We celebrate events and accomplishments both big and small. Weddings, graduations, and the birth of a child are all big events that help us share both our accomplishments and joy. These events are big and planned and always very special.

Celebrations for smaller things are not always such a big production, but they can be just as important. Think about your family and the way you celebrate life's little wins. If Cathy brings home three A's on her report card, she is given a dollar for each one. If Mike is in a piano recital, he gets ice cream afterward. Birthdays are other landmark events that most families honor with special traditions. In addition to the obligatory cake, the birthday boy or girl might get to eat off a special plate, choose what Mom makes for dinner, or decide to skip all of that and go to a restaurant. And how many of life's little events have you celebrated at your own kitchen table with a simple pizza and a lot of laughs? Was the good time you had or the love you felt any less important simply because there wasn't a lot of fanfare? Of course not!

It really doesn't matter what events take place or how the festivities play out; the important part is that we are celebrating these milestones together. Whether it's a first Little League home run or receiving a law degree, something good happened and we need to acknowledge it and feel great about it. These celebrations aren't just fun. They're an important way for you, your family, and friends to strengthen your relationships with one another.

Celebrations in the workplace are just as important. After all, most of us spend more of our waking hours with our coworkers than we do with our families!

Much has been written about reward and recognition in healthcare, but not enough attention is paid to celebration. In healthcare we work very hard, not just as individuals, but as teams. We accomplish great things, but we rarely celebrate those achievements. I am still waiting for the Oscars or Emmys for healthcare. C'mon, we deserve to be on TV, don't you think? Now, I know some of you are thinking that I have lost my mind, so I will tone it down a notch! Okay, back to reality.

The bottom line is that workplace celebrations foster relationship building, improve morale, enhance retention, and encourage employees to achieve results. Smart leaders use celebrations whenever they implement change and set goals and objectives.

A Milestone Motivator—With BBQ Sauce!

First, let's take a look at achieving a positive change—an excellent opportunity for celebration! When I was Vice President of Patient Services at Holy Cross, we made some dramatic changes in our Mother-Baby service. We were serving a population with a great need for our services, but, unfortunately, we lacked an adequate number of physicians to provide the necessary care. We were also short on resources and had an inadequate facility.

So, we recruited more obstetricians, built a beautiful new Mother-Baby unit, and increased the team's training and development. Before long, we were delivering 60 babies each month—double the number of deliveries that had taken place in our previous Mother-Baby unit. Naturally, the team started saying, "We are twice as busy as we used to be so now we need more staff."

But the new unit was designed and staffed for 100 babies per month, which is about three deliveries a day and was the hospital's eventual goal for the unit. Despite their mutterings to the contrary, we knew the existing staff could easily meet that demand. They just needed to get used to the heavier workload and faster pace.

The director of the unit understood that if the team was focused on accomplishing a goal, they would be less fixated on the negative. So she asked the team to decide how they wanted to celebrate when they reached the new target. And for some reason, they decided that they wanted to celebrate delivering 100 babies with a barbeque rib dinner. They came to that decision in January, and within the next couple of months, they were well on their way to reaching the target.

Once the director knew how the team wanted to celebrate, she went into action. She researched restaurants and caterers and decided where the food would come from, how much they would need, and how they could get it delivered. She decided to host the dinner in a large meeting room in the hospital. (That way staff members who were working that day could take part in the celebration and those not working could come from home.) She worked with her team to pick out decorations for the room and music for entertainment. She asked key administrators to help serve the dinner.

So, the plans were all set. Then, months went by. In April, the monthly census increased to 98 deliveries. May was a heartbreaker with 99 deliveries. "We were one baby away from the ribs!" lamented one nurse. And then, finally, June was THE month! They started June 30th with 98 deliveries. By 6:00 p.m., they brought three more babies into the world. They had reached their goal and the team was ready to celebrate!

Now, if the director had not planned every last detail in advance, when do you think a team who hit their goal on June 30th would actually get their celebration dinner? Late July or August? Probably so, and at that point the celebration would have been meaningless.

Celebrations must be timely. Otherwise, they will fail. You would never tell a child, "Tommy, you did really well in the school play tonight. Two months from now, we are going to take you out for ice cream."

Prior planning is the key to meaningful and rewarding celebrations. And luckily the director of the Mother-Baby unit had everything ready to go. Her staff celebrated with their rib dinner on July 2.

Celebrate. Celebrate. Then (You Guessed It) Celebrate Again.

Successful teams know that creating urgency is vital to achieving benchmark results. And a celebration is a great way to create urgency.

Once the goal is set, the method for celebrating achieving the goal should be set as well. It is perfectly okay to have several different celebrations planned as various targets are met. It keeps people excited throughout the process.

Several years ago, one hospital was working on improving their patient satisfaction scores. They started their climb in the 30th percentile. The organization's leaders decided that although the ultimate target was to make it into the 75th percentile, they wanted to mark other milestones along the way in order to keep everyone motivated.

The plan was set. Once the 40th percentile was met, there would be a '40s swing party held in the cafeteria. The 50th percentile would be heralded with a jukebox and sock hop. When the 60th percentile was attained, there would be a Motown dance contest. And at the completion of the journey, the 75th percentile would be celebrated with a disco ball and all the trappings of the polyester-and-gold-chains era.

The team not only worked hard to reach each and every goal, but they were also able to take time along the way to celebrate their accomplishments and re-energize by enjoying that down time together. Celebrations help teams create urgency by keeping them focused and rewarding their efforts along the way.

Finally, celebrations help us with recognition. Staff reach milestones all the time. Why not recognize the years of service members of your team have put in by celebrating anniversary dates at the department level? Or, I know most healthcare organizations hold an annual service awards event, but why wait five years? (C'mon, you know it's true. No one ever gets that excited about those massive "annual" dinners anyway!)

Staff should be acknowledged every year at the department level. Maybe you're thinking, *But Liz, we don't have the budget for that!* To that I say, "You don't have to go hog wild!" It doesn't have to be a huge blowout. Think about your own family celebrations. Most of them are probably simple affairs, but they get the job done.

Perhaps on a team member's anniversary date, she gets to decide what assignment she wants for that shift or what time she gets to go to lunch. Flowers or food always work well too as do small gifts and cards.

And remember, you don't always have to do the same thing for everybody. Making things individualized and personal only makes the acknowledgment more remarkable. For example, if Marcy has a favorite sports team, a cake with the team's colors would make her celebration even more special.

Ask team members what other things they would like to celebrate. It can be practically anything. In fact, I know of one team that gets candy any time they go an entire week without any member calling in sick. Or maybe people want to celebrate educational accomplishments or personal ones, such as professional certifications or acquiring healthy habits.

The great thing about celebrations is that they are an aspect of work that we can all like. After all, do you ever begrudgingly enjoy a good dinner or a piece of cake?!? It's almost impossible to not have some sense of enjoyment, and if you can eat that cake without any joy, well, then, I'm not sure I can help you!

Celebrations, by definition, are an expression of joy. Start weaving them into your workplace, and I believe you will find that their benefits are endless. We all deserve to feel great about the work that we do. After all, we are the only ones who really know how tough it is to do what we do and achieve what we achieve day in and day out.

We need to celebrate our accomplishments. It will not only help us to reach our goals and be better teams, it will also serve as a reminder about the great things that happen in healthcare every day. It will help us stay focused on what is right about healthcare.

11

Destination Unknown: How to Get Control of Your Career Destiny

If we are going to create positive work environments, it is essential that each member of the team understands that they are in control of their professional destiny. I learned this while I was working outside the hospital environment.

Most people don't know that in between ED management jobs, I tried two other professions. The first was as a utilization review nurse for a large insurance company. I hated it! Not the work so much as the environment. We had to sit at desks all day long, in rows of cubicles. We weren't supposed to talk to each other, and we had to keep track of every minute on these log sheets. And I mean every *single* minute. If we got up to go to the bathroom or get coffee, we had to log it in as "I" and "O." That's "intake" and "output" for you non-medical folks. I think I lasted about 120 days there.

I was also a headhunter! Okay, professional recruiter. I became one after I went to work for a great man named Matt Hale. He owned several executive search firms that specialized in accounting, data management, and general computer work. He wanted to start a firm for healthcare, and he hired me. We hit it off very well. He liked my talkativeness, and I enjoyed learning from him.

I stayed with that company for three years and truly enjoyed the work. But I missed being on the inside of healthcare. Even though all of my clients were hospitals, I always felt like I had my nose pressed up to the glass looking in from the outside. One day I made a sales call to Holy Cross to see if I could get the job listing for the Emergency Department director position they had open. As the HR manager told me about the position, I thought, *I would be great at that job.* And, well, you know the rest of the story.

One concept that Matt taught me was that everyone should be in control of their working future. He also mused that most people are not.

Most people give very little thought to the future of their careers. He said most of us just kind of bob along hoping to be happy at work, but we usually don't find all that much to be happy about. And then we blame that unhappiness on other people at work, such as the boss or our coworkers.

What's the Plan, Man?: The Importance of Career Planning

It was Matt who enlightened me about the fact that most people spend more time planning a one-week vacation than they do planning their other 49 or 50 weeks at work. I always remembered that. It stuck with me. Maybe because I was guilty of it myself.

I used to show up at work hoping that the organization had "Please Liz" on its to-do list every day. And then when they didn't, I complained. Sometimes I dreamed of doing different work in a different environment, but I never took much action. It was a lot easier to just moan and complain about the status quo.

But as the story goes, things changed for me and one day early on in my speaking career, I was asked to do a talk on morale. I decided as part of the presentation I would expound on Matt's theory. *Do people really spend more time planning their vacations than they do their careers?*

Well, I know this: People *do* spend a lot of time planning a vacation. Nobody wakes up on the first day of their vacation saying, "Where should I go? I hope I end up somewhere nice! I hope there are a lot of things to do. I have been anticipating this time for awhile, and I can't wait to get started!"

People don't just get in their cars or go to airports and get on a plane. Destination? Anywhere! We plan our vacations. We research places we want to go. We listen as other people talk about their travels, and we make mental lists of possible destinations. Sometimes we include others such as our family and friends in choosing the destination. And once we agree on the destination, the actual planning begins. Family vacations are always so well planned because the planning itself is a fun activity.

We set a budget, search for flights, and research hotels online. Some of us arrange for side trips. We even look for interesting facts about the location.

We heavily research the main reason for choosing the destination, whether it is a major amusement park, urban Mecca, or relaxing beach. A few of us plan the trip by day—what and where we will be each day and what needs to be in the itinerary so that we can ensure that all travelers will have a good time.

And then there's the food. Food is an important part of any trip. Lots of folks spend hours on the Internet or reading books about restaurants at their destination. We want to find local favorites, those with five stars, or the ones with great views of the sunset. My husband, Frank, even likes to look at the menus ahead of time.

I think you get the idea. Most people spend between 8 and 20 hours planning their vacation. But hardly any of us spend even an hour a year planning our careers. And that not only holds us back from being happy at work, it also limits our options.

Your Future's So Bright...

Here is an example I often share. When I was about 26, I thought about changing careers. I really thought I wanted to work in marketing. And I was pretty serious about it for maybe a day. I looked into a position that was posted at our hospital for an entry-level marketing position. But I didn't look long, because when I saw the salary I stopped. At that point in time I was earning about $28,000 a year, and the marketing position paid only $18,000. I remember telling my friend, "I would love to work in marketing, but I can't. I need the money. I can't take a $10,000 pay cut! I am trapped in golden handcuffs!" All right, that is a little dramatic, but that's the way I felt at the time.

But the truth was I wasn't a victim of the hospital. I was a victim of my own lack of planning. Instead of whining, I should have been planning, and the plan could have gone like this:

First, I should have chosen my destination carefully. Once I decided that marketing was that destination, I could have started volunteering for small projects in the Marketing Department—maybe staffing a health fair booth or writing an article for the newsletter. After doing a couple of them, I could have then participated on an organizing committee, perhaps the team that plans the hospital's annual open house.

I could have continued this pattern for a couple of years. Participating and volunteering for committee work, and all the while getting to know the staff of the Marketing Department. I am sure that sooner or later I would have been able to chair a committee. Again, starting with a small one and then working my way up to bigger responsibilities. Had I done all of that and had a position then opened up in the Marketing Department, not only would I have been qualified, but the principals in the Marketing Department would have already known me and my skill set. I may not have had to start at an entry-level salary. I might have been able to make a lateral move salary-wise, and then poof, the "golden handcuffs" are removed.

Now some of you might be saying, *But I don't like what I am doing* right now. *Wouldn't five years be too long to wait?* Well, maybe if you just do nothing for five years and wait for things to happen to you. But that is not the case with the person who plans. That person would have followed the above example and would have started feeling energized as soon as the destination was decided.

Choosing a destination is the beginning of the journey, and from that moment on, you are in control of your destiny. You can arrive in the blink of an eye, but you have to have a plan, a road map. And it is that road map that helps us understand that we are not victims; we are in charge of our career's future.

And I know some of you are already thinking, *What if I volunteer on a couple of projects and hate it?* It doesn't matter, because it is much better to find out before you make a major change. That way you are still in control.

Is the Grass Really Greener?

And here is another way that we can be in control of our destiny. I used to suggest to everyone who worked for me to go out and do a job interview once a year. In fact, I did it myself. You might think it sounds crazy, but it is not. There is a rhyme to my reasoning here, I promise! It is good to get out there and see what is available. It gives us perspective of our own strengths and weaknesses. I remember once I was on a group interview for a position, and two people in the group asked me what I had published. Wow, I can tell you that question stopped me from thinking that I was God's gift to healthcare.

Some of us think we could go anywhere and get hired. Other people are terrified to even think about interviewing. Those are the people who need to do it the most. Because in the back of their minds, they might be thinking, *I would like to do something different, but I can't imagine going through the interview.*

I used to advise those people to interview before they "needed" to. Most of them never left their jobs, but they at least knew they could get past the first and highest hurdle.

And there were always those people who looked at new opportunities and immediately came up with reasons that they didn't even want to interview. "It's too far," I heard. "It's in a bad neighborhood," they said. "My friend worked there and said they work people to death," they said. When I was a professional recruiter, I used to tell candidates all the time that they didn't have a decision to make until they actually had an offer.

What does all of this have to do with controlling your destiny? Simple, it puts you in charge. It keeps you sharp, and it gives you a realistic view of your career options. Most people who interview like this don't leave their jobs, but what they do is make a conscious decision to stay.

Let's say they get an offer, and now, as I said before, that is when they truly have a decision to make. If they turn the offer down, then they are saying to themselves in a very big way, *This is where I belong now. This is the best job for me at the present. I WANT TO BE HERE!*

Think about working with a whole team of people who every year make the choice to work in your departments. I guarantee you there would be a lot less negativity. I hope all of you will take this advice and commit to spending a minimum of eight hours a year planning your own career.

Here are some things to think about as you do so:

Where do I really want to be five years from now?

If I don't know, what will help me get a better idea?

What do I like the best about my current job?

What is the worst thing about my job?

What job/career would make me excited to get out of bed every morning?

What do other people say I do really well?

What am I passionate about?

What drains me?

What resources could help me (Internet, other people, books)?

12

Do Unto Others: How Committing to Kindness Will Improve Your Workplace

On the day I got married, my father walked me down the aisle, and as he lifted my veil he started talking to me. His words were very sweet, too sweet in fact. As he was talking to me, I was on the verge of the ugly cry, and when he said, "I hope you have half as much happiness in your life as you have brought your mother and me," you guessed it: By that time, I am in the midst of a full-blown, ruin the salon-applied makeup, major ugly cry. So I told him to stop. Well, I didn't actually say the words because I couldn't speak. So I started waving my hands like a crazy person. Yeah, I know, not a pretty picture for a bride!

Having learned from his experience at my wedding, Dad took a different, slightly safer approach when my sister Donna got married. He kept his advice short and sweet. As he lifted her veil, he gave what I believe is the best advice *ever* given to a newly married couple. His words were brief but very profound. He told her, "Be kind to each other."

How brilliant! Love, passion, companionship—all of those things are impossible without kindness. Obviously, it is not easy to be kind all the time to the person you married. Frank and I have been married 27 years, and there is a reason my mom calls him Poor Frank. (To be fair, she also refers to Donna's husband as Poor Tom!) It is a struggle to do everything with kindness. But just like marriage itself, committing to kindness is a commitment worth making.

And more of us should be making this commitment at the workplace. There is a tremendous shortage of kindness at work. Sometimes it almost feels like we are going out of our way to be unkind to each other. We most certainly don't go out of our way to give anyone a break. It is tough, and day after day, it breaks us down as individuals and as teams.

Falling into the Workplace Rivalry Trap

It is foolish to think that our lack of kindness doesn't affect our work environment. In fact, when people leave their jobs, the most common reason given for their leaving is that it's because of their boss or their coworkers. Through kindness, we *can* make a difference with team members.

Boy, we are tough on each other! We make judgments very quickly, and once we share those bad thoughts with others, they really escalate. Sometimes the bad feelings are felt by all parties involved and nobody even knows why. Kind of like the Hatfields and the McCoys. When I was a new nurse, it was based on what weekend you worked. Back then everyone worked every other weekend, so it turned out that the same people would always work together the same weekend. And each of the weekend teams had very strong opinions of their group and the other group.

I remember being put on my weekend schedule after I first started in the ED. I worked a couple of weeks, got through orientation, and then I worked my first Saturday. At lunch two of the nurses filled me in on what I needed to know. "You are lucky you are on the good weekend." (Like I had a choice!) "All the hard workers are on this weekend (good so far), and we know that you are going to fit in just fine." (Phew, I was worried. Wouldn't want to be banished to the other weekend!) "All the fun people are on this weekend too…." (Yeah, I could tell. I was having a blast!)

But then I had a scary thought: What if fate had put me on the other weekend? MY LIFE COULD HAVE BEEN RUINED! Really? Nah, probably not. In fact, the other new nurse who started orientation with me, who by the luck of the draw was on the *other* weekend, said that her team told her the same things: "We are the fun weekend. We work harder, blah, blah, blah." It was one group against the other.

And that's how so many workplaces set themselves up. One weekend group doesn't like the other weekend group, day shift doesn't like the night shift, and the business office doesn't like the administrative assistants. This may all sound somewhat petty, and it is, but it is also dangerous because not only does it create a negative work environment, it also decreases the team's ability to function at its best. And usually that means that quality is compromised.

Shifting to Kindness

One time a hospital asked me to come in and work with a specific team of nurses. Their interactions with each other were dreadful, and it was most definitely affecting patient care. One issue was that the nurses on the late night shift (11:00 p.m.-7:30 a.m.) had very strong negative feelings for a nurse who worked the evening shift (3:00 p.m.-11:30 p.m.). We'll call her Laura. When I was conducting a focus group with the night shift nurses, they all started complaining about Laura. When I asked them to get specific, they told me, "She is a terrible nurse!" Wow, that is a pretty strong sentiment! And if it was true, it needed to be addressed with the departmental leadership.

But before I brought it up to the leaders, I met with Laura. We talked about a lot of things. She told me her background. It was rather impressive. She had many years of experience, had been a charge nurse at the hospital where she last worked, and she had been going to school working on an advanced degree but put it on hold when she started having children. She told me that she had a five-year-old son and a three-year-old daughter. She went on to tell me that she chose to work the evening shift because her husband worked the night shift at his job and on the days they both worked, they had to get a sitter for only a couple of hours to cover the time between when her husband left and she got home.

Laura seemed like a lovely person to me—committed to her family, bright, and hard working. I had a hard time believing that she was a bad nurse. But because my curiosity was piqued, as I was interviewing her further, I asked her what she thought of the people who worked the night shift.

To my surprise she said, "I think they are terrible nurses."

"Why do you say that?" I asked.

"Because they care more about their looks than their patients. They start every shift spending time fixing their hair and putting on lipstick," she insisted.

Wow, I thought to myself, *that makes a whole bunch of bad nurses in this department.*

In my next meeting with the night shift, I didn't mention the hair and make-up, but I did ask them why they thought Laura was such a bad nurse. "It's simple," they started. "This place can be up for grabs, all kinds of busy, and no matter what is going on she is out the door at 11:30 sharp. She never stays to help us. She doesn't even care. Sometimes she leaves only having given us a very brief report on our patients. All she cares about is walking out that door at 11:30."

So things started to make sense. At that point I did get the leader involved, and we started with Laura. Her manager asked her, "Laura, why do you think the late night shift is more concerned with makeup than the patients?"

Laura answered very matter-of-factly, "Because most nights they don't come out of the lounge until 11:15 or 11:20 to take the report because they are all in the back primping themselves."

The manager continued, "That is interesting, Laura, because the late night shift thinks that you leave sometimes without giving a full report."

"That is true," Laura said. "I have to leave at exactly 11:30."

"And why is that?" the manager asked.

"Because I have to catch the bus at exactly 11:40 in order to make it to the train station in time to catch the last train home at 12:00 a.m. My husband works nights and my babysitter has to leave by 1 a.m. If I don't catch that last train, I don't have anyone looking after my kids." I could tell she was uncomfortable because she looked to the ground when she told the last part.

Now does that sound like a bad nurse to you? Of course not! That is just a concerned mother trying to do her best. But I don't think that just because the late night nurses like to hang out in the lounge for a few extra minutes before their shift makes them bad nurses either.

It's obvious that a lack of understanding and kindness had all of these people thinking very negative thoughts about each other. The issue was resolved when the manager pulled everyone together so that they could look at all sides of the story. The late night shift nurses agreed to get onto the unit at 11:00 p.m. sharp so that Laura could leave at 11:30 to catch her bus. Laura also agreed that on those nights when the place was crazy busy and they needed her to stay an extra hour she would ask the supervisor to give her a voucher for a cab to get home.

I'd like to say that all of their nursing skills immediately improved after this, but who are we kidding? Over time, though, things did improve.

All of this could have been avoided if these nurses had committed to kindness. If it was a kinder environment, perhaps Laura would have been comfortable letting her team members know her predicament. Perhaps in a more relaxed setting, Laura could have approached her team members about the extra time they were taking at the beginning of the shift. Perhaps they could have all gotten together to find solutions and compromises that could work for everyone.

There isn't any right or wrong here. All sides could have done a better job. Neither side ever thought they were part of the problem. Both of them saw the other side as the problem. Kindness was absent from all involved.

Being kind is not difficult. It doesn't require any money, any training, any real effort. You can start right away. The beauty of kindness is that it doesn't take the whole team. One person can truly make a difference.

In our nurse story, all it would have taken is one person, either Laura or anyone on the night shift, to be the first to extend kindness, and the entire issue could have been resolved.

All relationships require kindness—so do all teams. We spend around 2,000 hours a year with our coworkers. Given how much time we spend with them, a little bit of kindness can really go a long way. By committing ourselves to kindness, starting today, we can really make a difference where we work.

13

The Pursuit of Happiness: How Choosing to Be Happy Can Create a Positive Workplace

Happiness, like positivity, is a decision. It is a decision we make as individuals, teams, and leaders. For this chapter let's just assume that happy workplaces and positive workplaces are one and the same.

Happiness is not about always being cheerful nor is it a result of simply being clueless about all the bad stuff that is going on around you. No, it is a choice. It is about being content with what *is*. I think it is the Buddhists who say, "It is what it is." I used to think, *Well, duh!* but now I get it. Happiness is about accepting where you are, what's going on there, and what you are doing.

When Being Right Won't Make You Happy

When it comes to happiness, though, the reality is that there are times when you can be right or you can be happy, but not both. My sister Donna taught me this lesson about 16 years ago.

Now, most of you don't know my sister, but let me tell you, she is a lawyer and a good one! She is not a pushover, and, in fact, she has been fighting ever since she learned to talk. They say what gets you into trouble as a child makes you successful as an adult. Well, I used to get in trouble for talking too much… HA! Now, I earn a living speaking. Donna used to get in trouble for arguing. She always felt compelled to question authority, mostly with our parents. I was more of a schmoozer. I talked my way into getting what I wanted. Not Donna. "THAT'S STUPID!" is what my mother and father remember as being her favorite comeback.

And now she is an attorney. And although she doesn't litigate (argue) all that much anymore, it is her reluctance to take anything at face value that makes her successful.

Donna and her family moved to New York City about 16 years ago. Right after they moved, my husband and I went to visit. Frank and I were typical tourists, and Donna was our tour guide. She took us to see all the famous sites—Empire State Building, Carnegie Deli, Rockefeller Center, etc. It was at Rockefeller Center that she parked the car in a spot we had just seen a driver pull out of. She assumed it was a legit spot…not so. When we came out, the car was towed.

She was not thrilled, but she looked on the bright side. "No need to rush to the impound lot. The car is parked now. We might as well finish up, and we can go get it at the end of the day." So Donna, Frank, and I continued to tour the city on what happened to be Valentine's Day. When we were finished, we took a cab to the impound lot.

The place was as bad as you can imagine. Horrifically long lines, workers behind bulletproof glass, frustrated people everywhere, and not a single employee with a sense of urgency. As we took our spot in line I thought, *Uh-oh, this is going to get ugly.* We waited for a few minutes and then a few minutes more.

I was waiting for Donna to exclaim, "This is STUPID!" but she didn't so Frank and I followed her lead. We patiently stood in line. It was the early '90s so the video camera we had been using that day was of the 20-pound variety and poor Frank was holding it on his shoulder. (If you are too young to remember those first video cameras, look online or ask someone about them; it will be good for a laugh!)

We stood in line for a while and didn't move an inch. Donna noticed that some people would get all the way through the line but then if they had a question or a problem, they had to go wait in another line to go to a different window. (How stupid!) She saw this as an opportunity. She dodged over, and we followed her like baby chicks as she went over to the "Question" line. It moved a little faster and in about 10 minutes she was at the counter.

I stood behind her, secretly smiling about the fact that the poor guy behind the counter had no idea what he was in for. I waited for her to unleash a torrent of rage upon him, but it never happened. Instead I heard my sister talking in the most sweet, syrupy voice, "Could you please help me, sir? I am from Chicago, and my car has Illinois plates?"…He interrupted her, "Well then you have to have the title and the registration." She said, "Oh dear, I think they are in my glove compartment. What will I do?" Are you kidding me?!? I looked at Frank, wondering exactly who was inhabiting my sister's body, because it definitely wasn't her.

The man talked to her abruptly for the next few minutes, and at every moment was met with my sister's sickening sweet questions or wonderment. At the end, after he told her what to do, we were able to go to the car to retrieve the documents, and best of all, we got to go to the head of the other line once we had them.

When we were back in the car, safe and sound, on our way to dinner, I asked her, "Just what was all of that? You sounded like June Cleaver back there. Where were the fireworks? The indignation? The Donna I know?!?"

She looked at me and said in the matter-of-fact tone that I am so used to hearing from her, "Liz, they are stupid, and they had your car."

AHA! You can be happy or you can be right, but most times you can't be both. Had my sister complained to the impound lot workers about the terrible set-up, she would have been right. It was terrible! But she made the decision to let that go and make the best out of a bad situation.

We can all make the decision to be happy—to like our work, enjoy our patients, appreciate our coworkers, and relish the day. When we do so, we are also doing our part to make our workplaces as positive as possible.

Giving Nice a Try

Here is another story about making the decision to be happy. I don't think I need to provide a lot of detail in this chapter teaching you to decide to be happy. I am hoping that a couple of good stories will do the trick!

This is Anne's story. Anne is a nurse I worked with at my first job. She is an excellent clinician. One day a group of us were all out to lunch, and Anne was miserable. She said, "I can't stand the patients at the hospital anymore. The clientele is getting worse by the day. They are mean and nasty, and I am done dealing with them! I am going to quit! I have just had it!"

I said to her, "Anne, have you ever worked just one shift where you were nice to all the patients, no matter what?" She looked at me like I had two heads. I pushed on, "You should try it for one week."

"Are you nuts? Did you just hear me? They are awful and mean, and I am not going to be nice to them for a week!" she pushed back.

"What do you have to lose? You are going to quit anyway. Why not give it a try?" I asked.

"All right, I will," she declared. "But only to prove that you have lost your mind!"

"Great, how about starting this week?" I suggested.

"No way," she said. "I can't just go in there and start being nice to these miserable people. I have to plan it."

So she picked out her Nice Week, and she told everyone she worked with about the plan. *Good idea*, I thought, *because if she didn't people would have probably thought she needed a psych work-up.*

When the week arrived, she was nervous. In fact, at the time she told me that she thought it was going to be the hardest thing she had ever done in her career. *Really?* I thought to myself. *Going to work and being nice to the "mean" patients is going to be the hardest thing you have ever done.* Now, this is a woman who worked in a busy trauma center and had seen it all. Apparently none of that stuff fazed her, but going to work and pledging to be nice for one week was going to be the hardest thing she had ever done!

And so Nice Week began. Anne started her shift and starting with her first patient she knew she was going to be tested. The patient's chart read, "Thirty-two-year-old male complaining of a sore throat for two weeks." Now, if you are an ED nurse, you read that description and the theme song from *Jaws* or *Psycho* starts pounding in your ears. A sore throat should not warrant a trip to the ED. But Anne remembered her mission. She could be right in feeling as though the man had no business in a busy Emergency Department and express that notion to him, or she could experiment with this happiness thing.

She escorted the man into an exam room and instead of saying, "So, sir, what exactly makes this sore throat an emergency…TODAY?!?" she refrained and instead said to him, "I see on your record that you have been suffering with a sore throat for the past couple of weeks. That must be very unpleasant for you. After I'm finished getting your history, I will ask our doctor to come in and examine you. Now, before I leave, is there anything else I can do for you?"

The man quietly said, "No." The doctor examined him and wrote out his discharge instructions for the patient. They included fluids, rest, and Tylenol. And this was back in the day when we would get samples and could give them out. So Anne grabbed a big handful of Tylenol and went in to send the man home.

She repeated his instructions about fluids and rest and told him that the doctor wanted him to take Tylenol. She handed the man the samples saying as sweet as she could, "I didn't know if you knew where to get Tylenol (like you can't get it at a gas station) or if you had any at home, so here are some to get you started. Now, before I leave, is there anything else I can do for you?"

And the man said, "No, but I have to tell you something. I came in here today prepared for a fight. I know that I should have my own doctor, and I don't really belong in an ED. But I don't have a doctor, and whenever I am sick, I think about it but by then it is kind of too late. So I just thought, *I am going to the ED anyway, and if they don't like it, it is just too bad.* I was really prepared for the worst. But instead you have been so kind and so understanding. I just can't thank you enough. You have made what I thought was going to be an unpleasant situation into a wonderful experience. Thank you."

Now Anne is looking at this man stunned. She is trying to figure out what else she can give him. "Would you like this stethoscope? How about a blood pressure cuff?"

It was working already, but Anne didn't know it yet. Around lunchtime the curiosity had gotten the best of me, so I called her to see how Nice Week was coming along.

She said, "Liz, you won't believe it, but I picked the wrong week to be nice."

"How could that happen?" I asked. "It took you a month to choose this week!"

"I know," she answered. "But you know how your hair looks on the day you are getting it cut?"

Where is she going with this? I thought. But I played along. "Yeah, I know."

For those of you who don't know, and by that I mean all you males out there, it is a general rule that on the day you are getting your hair cut it looks great. It doesn't look great on the day you make the appointment; after all, that is why you call the salon in the first place. But one of the greatest mysteries on earth is why on the day you are scheduled to go in and have it done, you look in the mirror and think, *I could live with this. My hair actually looks nice.* DON'T FALL FOR IT! Most of us have, at least once. But it is a trick, because I guarantee that if you cancel the appointment, you can be sure that the next day your hair will look terrible.

But anyway, back to the story! I said to Anne, "What does this have to do with Nice Week?"

"It's the same phenomenon," she cried. "This is the week I decided to be nice to all these miserable people, and as luck would have it, everyone that I have taken care of today has been friendly and pleasant!"

Now, of course the clientele in that Emergency Department did not change over night. But what *had* changed? Anne! She made a decision to be happy. At first she didn't even buy into it. She was just doing it to prove me wrong, but it still worked because, like deciding to quit or deciding to be unpleasant to every rude patient or client you come into contact with, happiness is a decision.

Anne stayed in the ED for several years after that. During that time whenever the place was starting to get to her, she would throw in a day or two of abnormal niceness. Full-on sweet, over-the-top kindness. Imagine that! Imagine working in a place with people like Anne who pull themselves out of their bad moods rather than drag others into them.

If we are going to create positive work environments, we have to choose to be happy. We need to make the decision as individuals and as teams. Happiness is not just thrust upon us. It is something we strive for and work towards.

Try it, either as a team or just by yourself. Try having your own Nice Week and see how far it takes you in creating a positive workplace.

"It is our choices that show what we truly are,
far more than our abilities."

—J. K. Rowling

Accelerate the momentum of your Healthcare Flywheel®

SPEAKING ENGAGEMENTS:

Liz Jazwiec has a powerful ability to relate to all levels of an audience with her sincere, engaging delivery. She leaves you with good, practical takeaways... that work!

To schedule a speaking engagement, visit www.lizjazz.com or www.studer-group.com/speakers.

VIDEOS:

Watch a preview of Liz's video series titled *Heroic Service: Perfecting Perception*, developed to provide educational opportunities on service excellence for individual organizations at www.lizjazz.com.

RELATED ARTICLES:

Read "It's How One Looks at It" by Quint Studer—Quint talks about how Liz explains examples of how we can accept negativity without really knowing it. To read, visit *Quint's Corner* at www.studergroup.com.

INSTITUTES:

Attend "Taking You and Your Organization to the Next Level," a Studer Group institute where you can watch Liz live on stage along with other renowned national speakers who share their success stories and proven results.

To learn more about Studer Group institutes, visit www.studergroup.com/institutes.

To find out what institutes Liz will be speaking at, call Sheila Martin at 850-934-1099 or visit www.lizjazz.com.

Keep in touch with Liz and view current blogs and materials at www.studergroup.com/eatthatcookie.

Acknowledgments

My utmost thanks to the following:

Quint Studer, for being a great mentor who takes me to the next level every time I am with him, and for being the kind of dear friend who stays near me even when I am not with him. He has taught me, by his own example, that striving for excellence does not require perfection. We all contain within ourselves everything we need to be successful; reaching excellence simply requires the desire to make things better.

Mark Albarian, most importantly for a friendship that has carried me through the darkest of times. But also for being the kind of friend who celebrates my victories as if they were his own and for continuing to offer me unparalleled advice even though **EVERY** time he does so I (at least at first!) argue and fight him on every bit of it. Though I might go kicking and screaming, he always shows me the right way.

Bill Hejna, for being a truly amazing individual. The world of healthcare is lucky to have him. He is simply wonderful! Our camaraderie, which developed first as colleagues, has transformed into a true and deep friendship that has become one of my most valued and cherished.

Mark Clement, for not firing me! He is a second chances kind of guy. He saw my potential long before anyone else did (myself included). Mark pulled our team at Holy Cross out of the "victim-thinking" trap and taught us to embrace a no-excuses mentality. He pushed all of us to do our very best, and for that relentlessness I am grateful.

Don Dean, for saving my career at Holy Cross and always remaining a loyal and dear friend.

Bekki Kennedy, for making this book possible with her combination of patience, encouragement, advice, and the willingness to let me express myself. Her excitement with this project was evident in every step of the process!

Sheila Martin, for being such a strong ally and close friend during all of my experiences working with Quint.

Margaret Stanzell, for her friendship, support, and professional guidance.

Dottie DeHart and her team (Anna Campbell, Ashley Lamb, and Lindsay Miller) at DeHart & Company Public Relations, a professional group of editors who helped me, a first-time author, keep my true voice alive on every page while working with me to craft a message that will resonate with my readers.

To my dear nurse friends, Anne Williamson, Eileen Ring, Laurie Round, Madonna Scatena, Nancy O'Keefe, and Patti Gomez, you all provide me with inspiration, guidance, encouragement, and most importantly, some really great stories.

Matt Hale, for teaching me how to establish a business, connect with clients, manage expectations, and most importantly, always see the bright side of every situation.

Paul Marcus, for teaching me not to fear or sabotage my own success.

BG Porter, for providing me substantial support in my affiliation with Studer Group.

Craig Deao, for not only managing my ego, but balancing it with all the other speakers at Studer Group as well.

Bob Murphy, for being my best buddy in Pensacola and continuing to be a great colleague and friend.

Becky Anthony of the Iowa Hospital Association, for her sponsorship and recommendation of my work within her organization and other groups across the country. It's because of her that I've been blessed with opportunities to reach out to some truly great audiences. I have so much respect for her, and I couldn't ask for a more wonderful advocate!

Ruth Walton, RN, MS, for being an instant kindred spirit and a forever supportive fellow nurse leader. The stories, anecdotes, and laughs we've shared are priceless!

Kathleen Collins, for all you do to keep me coordinated, organized, on track, and most importantly, on the right plane!

Everyone at Parkview Hospital in Ft. Wayne, IN, the birthplace of the "cookie" story!

ABOUT THE AUTHOR

A nationally renowned speaker, strategist, and consultant, Liz Jazwiec consistently ranks amongst the best of the best amongst other speakers. The president and founder of Liz, Inc., she has shared her passion for leadership, engagement, and service with audiences across the country.

She's also been an Emergency Department director, executive search professional, organizational development leader, and vice president of patient care. Her work at Holy Cross Hospital is one of the reasons that the organization was recognized for its award-winning patient satisfaction.

Today she uses all her experience and expertise to inspire organizations committed to building a culture where excellence is driven by strong leaders and engaged employees.

Audiences describe Liz's presentations as uplifting, motivational, and fun. They also clearly respect her practical and experience-based style. You're sure to enjoy her creative and viable suggestions for addressing some of the difficult issues facing organizations today.

If You Liked "Cookie," You'll LOVE "Cupcake!"

Liz Jazwiec has done it again! Her second book, *Hey Cupcake! We Are ALL Leaders*, is as funny and inspiring as her first. In it, she explains that we'll *all* eventually be called on to lead someone—whether it's a department, a shift, a project team, or a new employee—and delves into the traits and skills needed to do it effectively. In her trademark slightly sarcastic (and often hilarious) voice, she provides learned-the-hard-way insights that will benefit leaders in every industry and at every level. Readers will learn:

- How to GET OVER IT and help your employees get over it, too (Liz coins a new phrase, "Pink Robe Rage")
- Liz's amusing approach to managing change (it involves the acronym BARF)
- How to deal with problem employees and button pushers (Evil Queens, Wicked Poisoners, Calamity Janes, and more)
- A quick and easy "test" that will help you hire the right people
- How an ugly red nightgown can teach us to *tell* others what we really need

To order *Hey Cupcake!* at a special bulk discount rate, please visit www.firestarterpublishing.com or call 866-354-3473.

How to Order Additional Copies of

Eat That Cookie!
Make Workplace Positivity Pay Off... For
Individuals, Teams and Organizations

and

Hey Cupcake! We Are ALL Leaders

Orders may be placed:

Online at:
www.firestarterpublishing.com
www.studergroup.com

By phone at: 866-354-3473

By mail at: Fire Starter Publishing
913 Gulf Breeze Parkway, Suite 6
Gulf Breeze, FL 32561

(Bulk discounts are available.)

Eat That Cookie! and *Hey Cupcake!*
are also available online at www.amazon.com.